FOUR POUNDS OF PRESSURE

A MEMOIR OF RAPE, SURVIVAL, AND TAKING BACK MY POWER

DANIELLE LEUKAM

AUTHOR NOTE

*The events in this book are expressed to the best of my recollection
from the worst morning of my life, "That Morning."
Some names have been changed to maintain privacy, including the
perpetrator.*

*Trigger Warning: This memoir contains graphic descriptions of
sexual assault.*

Opinions are my own and not the views of my employer.

Cover Design by: Med City Creative - https://www.
medcitycreative.com
Cover Photographer: Twelve Ten Photography – https://www.
1210.photography
Edited by: Brooke Warner – https://brookewarner.com
Edited by: Amy Briggs – https://www.amybriggsauthor.com
Blurb written by: Christine Weimer with Our Galaxy
Publishing www.ourgalaxypublishing.com

This book is dedicated to my son.
All of the strength, courage, and bravery I possess
comes from simply being your mother.

May this memoir be someone else's survival guide.

Fellow survivors:
It is time we take back our bodies.
It is time we love ourselves.
It is time we take back our voice.
It is time we take back our power.

PROLOGUE

I have been targeted, terrorized, and wronged too many times by means of sexual violence and harassment. Rape culture needs to stop. People need to be made aware of and educated on rape culture so we can bring it to an end. So here I am. Stepping up to advocate against sexual violence with my experiences and what I have learned from them.

I am taking back my power and body, and I'm here to empower others to do the same.

It takes an average of four pounds of pressure to pull the trigger on a 9mm handgun. I was four pounds of pressure away from losing my life in the early morning hours of November 18, 2018. Can you imagine someone loading bullets into a magazine then loading it into a gun with the intent of pointing it at your head, demanding you cooperate? I can't either. But it happened. I was held hostage in my home at gunpoint, zip tied, and raped with my son sleeping in the room next door.

Here is my story.

FOREWORD

That morning, time didn't pass quickly enough.
I wanted it to be over.
I felt like I was counting down the last minutes of my life.
I felt like I would never be able to see my son again.
He was in the room across the hall,
Less than twenty feet away.
So close, but unreachable.

What if I never got to hear the pitter-patter of his bare feet on the floor again?
Or watch his chest rise with each breath as he slept so peacefully,
Or felt his heartbeat when I hugged him close?
It was the only thing keeping me going,
Keeping me smarter than him,
Doing what I needed to do and saying what I needed to say...
To survive.

And now, after that morning,

Every minute has been a gift and a blessing,
Like seeing stars when you stand up too fast,
But for every second of every day.
It's magic in the air,
And every moment will no longer be taken for granted,
Doing what makes me happy.
A second chance will do that for a person...
It's exhilarating.
It's beautiful.

That morning was not the end of me,
But rather, just the beginning.

Please do the same.
Cherish your time,
Do what makes you happy.
You never know if you'll make it through the night.

Seize the day, my friends.
Make right now,
Your new beginning.

1

November 18, 2018... *That Morning.*

6:15 a.m.

My iPad showed me it had been nearly five hours since the last time I looked at a clock.

My three-year-old's patience for having to stay in his room ended abruptly, and he begged me to let him go out to the living room. "Okay, honey, but Mommy is going to go first," I finally gave in. I snuck out of my son's bedroom and looked around while quickly grabbing my robe to cover my half-naked body.

My senses were on high alert for anything out of the ordinary as I cautiously turned on the lights. James bounced out behind me like it was just another Sunday morning. I made it to the kitchen, grabbed a steak knife from my cutting block and slipped it into the sleeve of my robe without him noticing.

"Mommy, why is there sugar on the floor?" he asked referring to what appeared to be Carpet Fresh covering the bathroom floor.

"That's not sugar, honey. That must be Carpet Fresh to

make the floor smell pretty. Maybe the worker-man thought the shower was stinky, so he put down this smelly stuff."

This is when I noticed my bedding in the tub and the shower curtain pulled wide open. "Honey, look what the worker-man did to our shower. He put all of Mommy's sheets in there. Look, honey. I wonder why he did that." I wanted to get James to notice. But why? To verify that this wasn't an endless nightmare? Maybe I wanted him to see it in case the man took everything out of my tub after we left. I needed a second set of eyes to witness this real-life nightmare and unfortunately the only person who could was my three-year-old little man.

James didn't say much before heading to the kitchen to crawl onto the counter for breakfast. I was afraid to let him out of my sight. I was afraid to go into my bedroom. I was afraid to touch my cell phone. I was afraid to do anything other than pretend like it was just another ordinary morning. The man, the monster, the rapist... He was in my house for so long, I wasn't sure if he had bugged it or put up hidden cameras to watch us. Was he downstairs listening, waiting to attack again?

"Sweetie, what do you want for breakfast?" I asked as I opened the fridge, trying to come up with a plan to get us out of the house.

"French toast sticks," he replied. He got out the toaster and put it up on the counter. While his pull apart EGGO French toast sticks were warming up, I put on *Paw Patrol* and snuck downstairs, knife still tucked in my sleeve, to make sure he wasn't down there. My heart was racing; my breathing was labored. Sweat was pouring from my skin as I rounded the corner and tip-toed my way down the stairs.

I didn't see him. What I saw was Carpet Fresh on the floor in every room. I saw my laundry basket at the bottom of the stairs, gun parts still in it, covered with Carpet Fresh. I saw the screen from a basement window lying on the floor. *This is where he came in.* I was afraid to get too close. I didn't venture far from the stairs; all I wanted to see was that he wasn't down there.

The coast appeared to be clear. I went back upstairs and said, "Mommy wants yogurt for breakfast. Let's go to the store to get some. And Mommy wants fresh coffee. We should go to the coffee shop too." I was stuttering, mumbling, trying to make words into sentences. I didn't shower, nor did I change my shirt. I went to the bathroom knowing I might be wiping away evidence, but I knew there was enough evidence inside that would still be there for the taking. I changed from my robe into a sweatshirt on top of my pajama shirt, brushed my hair, slipped the knife into my sweatshirt sleeve, and put on under-wear and jeans. I didn't see my green shorts I had worn to bed anywhere.

I grabbed my cell phone charger and snuck it into my sweatshirt pocket. I didn't want to be obvious that I was packing to never come back just in case he was watching. I snuck my morning medications and contact lens case into my purse. I had grabbed underwear and socks for James but ended up taking them out. I needed to be discrete.

I tip-toed to the garage, steak knife in hand, to grab James's tablet from my SUV. My mind was going in a million directions. I noticed the garage car-door was wide open. I didn't see anyone around, but I did see the man's footprints going down my driveway into the street. There was a light dusting of snow deep enough to catch his footprints, and there they were, right there in the damn driveway. Despite seeing his trail going away from my house, I still feared he was watching, waiting for any reason to finish what he had started.

I brought James's tablet into the house and took pictures of things the "worker-man" did. I had to explain to James whose voice he heard only an hour prior, and who was running water in our bathroom, so I told him it was someone fixing the shower. I took a picture of the tub, the marks on my wrists from the zip ties, and my husband Cody's gun case on my bedroom floor covered in Carpet Fresh. We were still married but had been separated for a year. I used the tablet because I was afraid to turn on my phone. I don't recall why I didn't use *my* iPad, but I did use it to look up the local grocery store's hours.

Score!

Mike's Grocery Store in St. Charles opened at seven a.m. By this time, it was just past seven o'clock, and somehow my heart was racing even faster as I got James into pants and shoes. Perhaps it was the anticipation of freedom.

I put on a coat over my sweater, still carrying the steak knife. I held James in my arms tight against my body as we walked to the garage. I checked the far back of my SUV to make sure no one was hiding there. No one was there, so I put James into the car seat and strapped his seatbelt. *Did he bug my car? Is he going to follow us?* We had to act normal—just going on a quick car ride to the grocery store...

"Okay, we're headed to the store. Mommy needs some breakfast," I verbalized like I was putting on a show. The plan was to call my mom when we got there. I thought we could talk about what happened and figure out what we should do. Whatever we were going to plan needed to revolve around James's safety. *Should I risk our lives and call the cops? Should I pretend like it never happened? But what if he comes back?* Some of these thoughts were irrational and impractical, but priority number one was keeping my son alive. The man's threats sliced me like a knife, and I feared he would act on his promises of murdering us when I considered telling the police. Truthfully, it was *not* an option on my list of "what the hell do I do now," but telling my mom was.

I started my SUV and backed out of the driveway. The tires drove over the snow, but I didn't care if I ruined the evidence of his footprints. All I cared about was my son's breathing, his rosy cheeks, and his innocent brown eyes looking at me, his mommy, assuming he was safe. I felt his heartbeat through my own. Seeing him alive was the only thing I could comprehend, and it was the only thing that mattered.

I closed the garage door as I backed into the alley. Should I have went to a neighbor's house instead? Maybe. I drove away from our home with no intention of ever going back. I turned left out of the alley, another left, and a right onto Highway 14, closing in on freedom. As we made our way up the highway and past the John Deere on the right, I felt a slight tickle of relief. I saw the sunrise like I was just opening my eyes for the first time in my life. I was thankful to be alive with my little man. It was a feeling I will *never* forget.

At the same time, I was trying to make sure I wasn't being followed. I peered in my rear-view mirror making sure no one was there. When we got to the store, I left my purse in the car, grabbed my wallet, and we quickly went inside to "shop for breakfast." James grabbed a small cart like he always did, and we made our way through the produce section. The only shoppers I saw were male; I couldn't trust anyone. I was waiting to run into a woman, mindlessly throwing things into the cart.

As we rounded the corner to the second aisle, I finally saw a woman shopping. Again, *score!* My heart leapt with more anticipation. When we approached her, I calmly asked, "Ma'am, can I please use your phone?" I did have my phone with me, but I was still afraid to use it.

"Oh, sure," she said. She kindly handed me her phone and started talking to my son while I made the phone call to my mom. I stepped a few feet away so she wouldn't hear our conversation. My heart sank when my mom didn't answer, so I left a voicemail that said something like, "Mom, it's me. I need you to answer your phone." When I hung up, I called back immediately. She answered.

"Mom, it's me. *Listen.* I need you to load a gun, put it in your purse, and meet me at Mike's Grocery store, in the bathroom.

Bring Dad, bring your phone and Dad's phone," I whisper-yelled these demands at her.

"Honey, I can't do that," she said, referring to bringing a gun into a grocery store. "Do I need to call the cops?" she questioned. My mom was always so practical.

"No. Just do it. Mom, listen to me. Just do it, please! *Please, Mom!*" I begged. She must have heard the fear in my voice because she agreed to come as quickly as she could.

I handed the phone back to the lady and thanked her in the calmest tone I could manage. *How much did she hear? Does she think I am crazy?* But I honestly didn't give a damn.

It seemed like an eternity that James and I wandered around the store putting random items I had no intention of buying into our small cart.

"Mommy, can I have this ice cream?" James asked.

"Yeah, of course, buddy."

My parents' house was only about five minutes away from the grocery store, but it must have taken a while for Mom to load my handicapped father into the car. Finally, while we were in the frozen-food aisle, I saw a flash of purple walk by, heading towards the women's bathroom. I recognized Mom's posture and quick pace; I also knew she left Dad in the car because he couldn't get around without his scooter. I picked up James without saying a word and we ran to the bathroom following my mom. She was standing in the corner waiting for us. When I got into the bathroom, my body was convulsing. I couldn't speak. I hated myself for putting any responsibility on James—he shouldn't have had to be any part of this, but in that moment, all I could do was crouch down by him and say, "Honey, tell Memaw what the worker-man did. Tell her what the worker-man did to the bathroom."

He didn't say anything; all he seemed to focus on was the

fear in my eyes and the trembling in my voice. I stood and looked at my mom, and as I fell into her arms, I became hysterical. I was inconsolable and stomping my feet like I was in a marching band. I was hyperventilating and sobbing but somehow managed to speak the words that pushed my mom into action, "He had a gun and he raped me and he's going to kill us!"

I can't tell you how my mom felt at this moment, but all I know is she held me tighter than she ever has before while she grabbed her phone and dialed 911. I heard the horror in her voice when she cried, "Oh, honey. Oh, honey. Oh my God!"

"No! No! He's going to kill us!" I screamed, trying to stop her from making the call.

James was crying, pulling at my coat looking up at me, "Mommy? Mommy?!" With every bone in my body and every ounce of my heart, I believed the man who threatened to kill us would follow through on his promise. For all I knew, he was out there in the grocery store waiting to make a move. But it was too late, the police were already on their way.

James was still hysterical, "Mommy! The worker-man hurt my mommy," he said to Memaw as he pulled up my coat sleeve to show my mom the marks on my wrists from the zip ties.

I don't want to die! He'll know. I had not kept my word that the police wouldn't find out what he did. These thoughts consumed my mind, but there was no going back now.

2

I THOUGHT SINGLE LIFE WAS GOING TO BE THE LIFE FOR ME. I didn't want to be with anyone else. I wanted to be alone and stand on my own two feet as my Aunt Lisa always taught me to do. The devastating heartbreak of drifting away from the love of my life was one I didn't want to endure again, so my plan was to not put myself in that situation.

Unfortunately, as soon as I became single, I appeared to be a damsel in distress or simply an object there for the taking. It's like abusers could smell my vulnerability. Being single sucked. Every time I was assaulted or harassed, I wondered, *Why does this keep happening to me? Why am I such an easy target?* I kept quiet about nearly everything to maintain normalcy in my life, but what I later realized it did was that it maintained normalcy in *their* lives also.

One of the few things that *always* made me feel better, gave me energy, empowerment, and strength, was running or going to the gym. I switched from the Rochester Athletic Club to Cutting Edge Fitness in St. Charles for convenience of location. The owner happened to be my neighbor, and he said I could bring my little man with me while I worked out. As a single mom, I had no other choice. James and I went there three to four days a week. Lifting weights felt like part of me. It was part of my weekly routine and I hated missing the gym. If I missed too many days a week, my anxiety skyrocketed.

In August of 2018 I finally reached the point of loneliness in which I was ready to start meeting new people. I met a man named Brian who was handsome, buff, kind, and had a good career proving he was an ambitious person. He was also intellectually on my level, which was awesome. We were only able to see each other every other weekend because I wasn't ready for him to meet my son. I was surprised I was able to open myself up to seeing someone after separating from Cody. Sure enough though, I found myself keeping a distance and taking things extra slow.

2018 was supposed to be my year. I had settled into my job as a full-time charge nurse. I had a lot of friends and I got along with everyone. My thirtieth birthday party was one of the best nights of my life. My friends from work and I got fancied up and celebrated at the Tap House in Rochester. Lots of our coworkers met us there. My sister and her wife, Amy, came down from the cities and my friend Kassie came up from Texas.

We had cake, there were giant balloons, and countless memories. It was like a coming out party for finally being thirty. *Now I can start my life*, I thought. I danced all night long with my loved ones hoping the night would never end. I stopped drinking early and ended up taking care of my friends who had too much; I rarely let myself be in a position of obvious vulnerability like being drunk in public. I wanted to be sure I was in control of myself.

3

———

November 17, 2018

6:50 a.m.

"Mommy!"

I heard my sweet little man's voice and felt his little hands grab my gray comforter and pull. He was strong for being only three. He pulled himself up onto the bed, crawled his little body right up next to mine, wiggled his way under the covers and settled in.

"Mommy," he sighed. His subtle smile, soft voice, and warm snuggles were a portrayal of how safe and happy he felt.

I woke up thinking how great of a movie *A Star is Born* was and how I was so glad I got to watch it with my friend last night. That was when I decided James and I would go to *The Grinch* cartoon movie that day. We would sit in reclined seats snacking on popcorn and candy, snuggling under a blanket inside, staying warm from the cold, snowy November. I didn't go to movies often because I was too practical and spending that much money at a movie theater seemed like a waste.

After a short time cuddling in bed, James and I ate breakfast and started planning our day at the kitchen table where we spent every meal together. I went downstairs to finish up a few things in the bathroom I was redoing. It was okay when we bought it, but the work in there seemed to have been done very quickly and on a small budget. I wanted to give it some love and make it look nice. As I was grabbing supplies, I noticed a stain on the carpet in one of the rooms next to the bathroom. I hadn't noticed it before and wondered if the cats had gotten into something. I didn't give it much thought before going back upstairs where James was playing with his dump truck and skid-loader.

I showered, put on makeup, grabbed a blanket, and headed to town listening to Michael Bublé's Christmas album along the way. I was trying to ask him what snacks he was going to want when we got to the theater, but you know what kind of conversation that is with a three-year-old... "I want *all* of the snacks!"

I checked my phone before we went in and it showed a message from my aunt Lisa.

Hi, honey! Do you and James want to come ice skating with us tonight?

We're at a movie right now. We're going to run some errands then decorate for Christmas. Next time? I replied. I wasn't sure how much money I wanted to spend on renting ice skates and skating, on top of going to a movie. Instead, we would have an evening at home preparing for the holidays. As a mom who works five days and nearly forty-five hours a week, spending an hour both before and after work traveling, I had to use the weekends to be productive.

I was standing in line at the concession stand trying to figure out what would be the healthiest snack for James. I asked, "What do you want to eat, buddy?"

"Sour gummies!" he replied. Of course. But I wanted to be sure we got something that would take a while to eat so he wouldn't eat it all in the first five minutes of the movie.

Ultimately, I failed at keeping the snack healthy. "Kid's

popcorn and sour gummy worms, please." We found our seats, snuggled under the blanket, and munched on our snacks. And sure enough, James had to go potty in the middle of the movie.

When it was over, we headed to Shopko nearby to pick up new lights for our Christmas tree that was graciously given to us by Cody's mom. The tree had been up for a week already at James's request, but we were lacking a decent set of matching lights. In the past, I had been using one strand of teal and one strand of multi-colored lights. This year was the year I would finally get matching Christmas lights for the tree. Adulting at its finest, and I was excited.

I had to call my mom for advice. "Mom, how many strands of lights do you put on your Christmas tree? I don't know how many to get."

"We've been using four strands. Are you guys decorating today? Give James a kiss from Memaw," Mom said. I settled with picking two rolls of lights; I didn't want to overspend. Michael Bublé lulled James to sleep for a short nap on the way back to St. Charles.

Little Man helped me find an extension cord and together we walked around the tree strategically placing the lights on each branch. We decorated it with ornaments, new and old, putting the beloved ones James had made himself front and center. Decorating the tree together would be a tradition we'd continue every year. It was such a simple yet magical day.

After a late lunch we went to the gym where I captured a video of James dancing to rap music that was blaring from the speakers. It was shoulder and back day for me, and I was pumped. I increased the weight on all of my sets and finished the workout with box jumps—my favorite thing to do at the gym. If I could have afforded to have my own box at home, I would have.

James created his own obstacle course with the boxes I

wasn't using along with a few yoga mats. "Mom, wait!" he wanted to jump at the same time as me.

"Okay! Ready... go!" I was incredibly proud of him for being creative, active, and ambitious.

6:15 p.m.

After finishing my eighty, twenty-six inch box jumps, I enjoyed an amino acid post-workout drink.

"Mommy, since I was good, can we get ice cream?" he asked with those big brown eyes peering up at me.

"Oh, I suppose," I caved. We drove through the A&W drive-through to get a vanilla ice cream cone. I always got the first lick so the sides wouldn't drip. Well, that's what I told him anyway.

7:01 p.m.

"James, what time is it?" I asked.

"Seven. Oh. One," he read.

"Good job!"

"Time to watch *Paw Patrol!*"

"Yes, it is, buddy."

After one episode of *Paw Patrol*, I tucked him in bed with his pink book light clipped on the side of the bed, his *Paw Patrol* night light shining colorful paws on the ceiling, a touch night light, his glowing iguana named Sheldon, and his soft yellow blankie. Oh, and a fresh bottle of ice water. If I didn't grab one ahead of time, it would surely be on his list of ten or more things he needed to come out of his room for.

"Goodnight, my little man. I love you."

"Goodnight, Mommy!"

I sat down on the couch to finally have some mom time which included Netflix and one glass of Pinot Noir. I had peeked at the lock on the front door to make sure the dead bolt was locked; it was. I checked to make sure the garage door was closed and the lights were off; they were. I checked to make sure the patio door was locked; it was.

I sent a message to my sister Erin who was in Kuwait; she had been deployed and stationed overseas since Memorial Day. She slept during my afternoon/evening time, but I was able to message her on the Signal App before I fell asleep at night when she would be just waking up for the day. I was incredibly proud of her. My sister was a beast. She played women's football (was MVP and on the All-Star team), was a respected Correction's Officer at the women's prison in Minnesota, and was a Sergeant First Class in the National Guard.

With the kitties on my lap, I scrolled through Facebook, Instagram, and Snapchat to see what was happening in the world. It wasn't long before I slipped into bed because I was exhausted from a long, productive day. I sent Snapchats of my cats to my friend Anne and sipped wine next to my glowing, beautiful, oh-so-special Christmas tree. I was happy.

I went to bed around nine-thirty p.m.

4

November 18, 2018

1:27 a.m.

Ugh, why am I awake?

I grabbed my phone and scrolled through Facebook and Snapchat when I realized the time was far too unreasonable to be awake for the day. I reached over my right shoulder with my left arm to grab my tall silver Yeti-knockoff cup and took a drink of water. I set my phone down in its usual place on the corner of my nightstand and curled up to fall back asleep.

I heard a noise at the end of my bed and thought, *What are the cats doing down there?* I grabbed my iPhone and clicked the side button so the screen would light up. I sat up and directed it towards the end of my bed to see where the sound came from.

That is when I saw *him*.

The light revealed a man, who in the blink of an eye stood up from a crouching position raising his arms to point a gun straight at my head. And there he stood—the noise at the end of my bed—and commanded, "Don't move. Don't move. ... If you don't move, you will be fine."

I saw he was over six feet tall in black clothes, a mask

covering his face, black gloves, and held a two-toned gun I was looking down the barrel of. At the time, I was certain this was going to be the last moments of my life.

There was nothing else I could say but, "Okay."

With chattering teeth and shaking legs, I was instantly dripping sweat. Adrenaline coursed through my veins and sleep was now the furthest thing from my mind. The only thing that was consciously crossing my mind was James.

Does he know I have a son? Oh my God! Has he been in his room? Maybe if I don't mention my son, he won't know there is anyone else in the house. I didn't hear gunshots. I would have woken up to James screaming. Please, God. Please let James be okay.

The man demanded, in his aggressive, disguised voice, that I, "Lay down." And I did. "Roll over." Again, I did. I moved to my stomach with my arms at my sides as directed. He quickly and effortlessly put a knee on my bed and grabbed both of my wrists in one swift motion. He had them zip tied together so tight in a matter of only a few seconds. *Has he done this before?* He was obviously prepared. He knew what he was doing. He knew what he was after. Once he accomplished having complete control of me, he stood up and looked down at me. I laid there on my stomach, feeling the zip ties that were holding my wrists tightly behind my back making me a hostage. It seemed as though he was calculating his next move as if he was playing a game of chess.

He appeared to be satisfied with his success of being in complete control. *This is it. I am going to die.* He had come here to take me, rape me, or kill me. Or perhaps all of the above.

I COULD SENSE the adrenaline and accomplishment in every breath he took. I instinctively offered him to take anything he wanted. I offered my TV, anything in my house he wanted, and money. Instead, he grabbed my silver water cup wrapping his fingers around the top and asked, "What's in here?"

I turned my head to see what he was referring to. "Water," I managed to mutter, though my throat was tight with fear.

"I need to give you something so I can get outta here." Although I didn't see what he wanted to give me, I instinctively knew he meant drugs.

I tried to maintain my composure and replied in a quiet voice so my son wouldn't hear. "I can't take anything; I have to be able to take care of my son. He can't take care of himself."

Fuck, fuck, fuck. If he didn't know I had a son before, he does now.

The man contemplated what I said.

"How am I going to get out of here?" he questioned. I wasn't understanding why he didn't leave the way he came as he paced near the side of my bed.

"There's a shovel in my garage. Take it with you and drag it behind you so no one can see your footprints," I suggested. I tried to think of anything to get him to agree to leave. Here I was, trying to rationalize with an armed, masked man who was holding me hostage with my little boy—whom I was hoping with all my heart was still alive and well—sleeping in his bedroom next door.

The man paused for a brief moment and then said, "I've been waiting for years to be in this position." It was like a scene from a horror movie. These words pierced my ears and scarred my heart but left me with more questions. *What position? Holding power over me? Control of me? To be in the position to kill me? To rape me? To hurt me?* What kind of monster would be wanting to do this to me for years? It was an eerie feeling leaving me to wonder if I had been watched for years by someone wanting to do evil things to me. I realized in this moment he knew me, and I probably knew him. I hoped to

God that maybe if I paid close enough attention, I could figure out who he was.

"Who are you, sir? Why are you here?" I begged, although I knew in my gut he wouldn't answer the first question, and I already knew the answer to the second. *Me.* So many things made this obvious. Why would he have been in my room otherwise? Why would he have brought zip ties? Why would he have said he'd been waiting for years to be in this position?

"Do I know you?" I asked, and then I learned I shouldn't have. The whole time he had maintained a consistent, deep and gruff tone; it was almost like he had a device that was disguising his voice. But upon asking if I knew him, his voice grew louder and his words became more stern and quick, and he sounded as though he was nervous. He swiftly and angrily moved to the end of my bed. "Do you know who I am?" he asked. I remember this clear as day; he was two steps closer to the door than he had been previously.

"No." I could hear my voice shake. He didn't want me to know who he was.

He now yelled in the disguised voice, "You're lying!"

"I don't know who you are. That is why I am calling you, 'sir.' Please believe me!" I begged.

"How am I supposed to know you won't call the cops when I leave?" he demanded.

"Please, I won't! I promise. No one has to know you were here," I said, pouring my heart and soul into convincing him to believe me.

"You know I will be watching you when I leave. I will know if you call the cops. I will see you."

"I would rather be alive with my son tomorrow than tell the cops. Please. I want to watch him grow up to get married and be a star basketball player. I want to make snow angels with him in the morning. Please, believe me." I tried to paint a picture of reality for this monster. I needed him to see the life I wanted and *would* live with my little boy.

I figured he was asking me these questions of how he'd leave my house because it was a change of plans for him. It would have been much easier to leave if he had drugged me.

I rolled over onto my back with my wrists aching in pain behind me and for a third time begged him, "Take anything you want. You can take my TVs. I have money in my dresser drawer." I sat up and noticed sweat pooling on my legs and feet. All I had on was a bedtime T-shirt—one of Cody's old shirts, because I still was not over him—and my favorite pair of green shorts that were given to me from my aunt Lisa.

He crouched by the side of my bed. His closeness terrified me. He put an ungloved hand on my bare right thigh and asked, "What if this is what I want?" This gesture confirmed my initial gut feeling. *He came here for me.*

I had no words to reply to this. It made my whole body tense and shake with profound fear. I had goosebumps but was sweating even more than I already had been. I felt completely drenched. *When did his gloves come off?* I didn't know what he was going to do or how he was going to do it. I didn't know if he was going to kill me afterwards. *Why would he keep me alive? Where is his gun?* The sacred side of my bed I slept on every single night, the side I was currently on with my heart beating out of my chest, would forever be tainted.

I told him exactly where he could find money in my drawer, and he replied in a calm voice with his arms up on the side of my bed as if he was sitting at a bar waiting to be served. "You work for your money, you keep it." *Who is this man? Who breaks into a house with no intention of stealing money?*

There was silence following this statement as chills engulfed my body. He confirmed, yet again, he did not want material things from my home. I had a wad of money in the drawer, and he wanted nothing to do with it.

To break the moment of silence, I said, "Sorry for being so sweaty. I probably smell awful." My brain was trying to normalize what was happening; I was trying to connect with him. But adrenaline, nerves, fear for our lives and a pounding heart kept me grounded. I felt clammy from my feet, my toes, my shins and calves, my knees, thighs, torso, and all the way up to my head where tears continually streamed down my face.

He moved his position from crouching to sitting on the edge of my bed and was only a couple of inches from me now. He crawled over the top of me, forcing me to lay down with him on top. I was crushing my hands behind my back and I could feel the zip ties digging deeper into my wrists.

But I cooperated. What else could I do with my hands zip tied behind my back?

He stayed in this position for a moment, seemingly enjoying that he was in control and planning his next move. "I'm sorry I stink, I have like four layers on," he said. I couldn't smell anything, hardly ever, in fact. It was an unfortunate void I had for as long as I could remember. Besides, like I was honestly going to say, "Oh, it's okay." *Not.* And also, why did he have four layers of clothes on?

He moved his body closer and grinded his pelvis against me as I shook uncontrollably. I was becoming more terrified every second, knowing what was going to happen and knowing what he wanted. My mind was searching savagely for answers: *How the hell am I going to make it out of this alive? How the hell am I going to keep my son safe?*

I needed him to think I wouldn't tell anyone nor call the cops. If I screamed, no one would hear me except for my son. If I put up a fight, no one would know except him and my son, and the cops who would find my body the next day. The last thing in the world I wanted to do was to wake up my son and bring him into this situation. I knew it would turn ugly if he came into my room and saw that his mommy was tied up.

The man positioned his body to where he was laying on my left side. He pulled up his mask and kissed my lips twice. I could feel stubble of hair on his face. Leaning over the top of me now, he kissed the right side of my neck, then the left. He put his bare left hand on my right hip and ran his hand up under my shirt to my right breast. I felt like he was Mr. Freeze turning me into a cold, frozen, statue of a body. Helpless. Paralyzed. As his weight was on top of me, my wrists throbbed with pain, causing my hands to become numb behind my back. I tried to adjust. The man—the monster—reached around my back to feel my wrists. I said, "It's fine." I didn't want him to be any closer to me than he already was, and I certainly didn't want my back turned to him.

"Where are scissors? Nail clippers? Do you have any in here?" he asked. He got off my bed and walked towards my door.

"No, but I do in my bathroom," I explained. *Why does he want scissors? So he can cut these off and put on looser ones?*

He looked at me silently for a moment, seemingly contemplating what to do. Once he made his decision, he threatened in a stern voice, "Don't even think about moving."

"Okay." I cooperated. He went from quietly kissing my neck to standing and commanding things of me. His inconsistencies were frightening.

The bathroom was right next to my bedroom; the doors were adjacent to one another. Straight across from my door was James's door with the bathroom in between. He turned on the bathroom light and dug through the drawers. He could not find the scissors.

"They're in the drawer on the right, next to the clear organizer," I explained, sensing his frustration, and trying to sooth it before he became enraged.

When he found the scissors, he came back into the bedroom. "Turn around," he demanded. I complied.

He came onto the bed to cut them off. When my wrists were finally free, I instantly drew my hands to my chest. I was rubbing my wrists and covering my body as I sat freed and extremely nervous. I didn't want to move my arms away from my body; I didn't want to be exposed. I rubbed my feet together as a new set of nerves coursed through me. Having my hands and arms untied brought an entirely new feeling: freedom, but obviously not enough. I was in a better position to be able to fight or escape, but we both knew I was now more of a liability, and I did not want to die, so I appeased him.

He moved his body in such a way that caused me to lie down and before I knew it, he was on top of me again. I didn't want to make him upset even as he used my son as a pawn for my cooperation. I was afraid to disobey him for fear of what he would do to James. As I lay there, I was forced to listen as he continually threatened to kill him in that evil, disguised, sadistic voice.

I finally told him, "I would do anything to save my son."

"Prove it," he replied.

Or what? Is he going to shoot me? Is he going to strangle me? Is he going to go into my son's room as a threat? Is he going to shove the drugs he tried to get me to take earlier down my throat? Is he going to drug my son? Did he already drug my son? Cooperating at this point was working to my advantage. He hadn't drugged me or beaten me or shot me... yet anyway.

I didn't know where his gloves were. I didn't know where his gun was. I didn't know if he was going to rape me then kill me. The only thought in my mind was, *make him go away*.

This was when my green shorts were removed from my body and I was raped by this armed, masked, disguised monster of a human being. I needed him to go away and leave my son and me alone, to leave us alive. Tears silently drained from my eyes; each tear holding a piece of my worth, my pride, my heart, and my soul, creating a river of who I used to be on my face. My heart hurt and my head hurt. *How is this happening? Is this real life? Why me?*

I hoped to God he would leave after he got what he wanted. I wanted the threats to stop. I wanted my life back. I wanted my body back. I wanted to be free. I wanted him to get the hell away from James, out of my house... out of me.

He asked me, as though I was a casual friend, if I wanted him to stop. And even though I was afraid to upset him, I told him the truth, "Yes." *Of. Fucking. Course.* To my surprise, he stopped. He was silent for a moment lying next to me, then moved his position to the side of my bed.

My respite from his touch ended abruptly when he suddenly grabbed my legs, spreading them apart to rape me again. I couldn't scream. I couldn't push him off me for fear of making him mad. I didn't have a husband home to call out for. I didn't have anyone. All I had was myself, so I needed to figure it out on my own.

He was on the sacred side of my bed raping my lifeless body when I realized my eyes were adjusted to the darkness. I was able to notice some of his clothing. I disassociated with what was happening to me and obtained a clear mind; I needed to think productively. Noticing anything and everything would be vital, so I took mental note of every detail I could. In this position with him on top of me, I noticed his black Under Armor zip-up with a small white Under Armor logo on his left chest. There may have been a white stripe on the sweater going down the sleeves. I filed these details in my mind like I was taking notes for later use.

After a few minutes he suddenly stopped. He pulled out of me from the straddling position he was in and pulled up his pants: jeans with a belt, and sweatpants over the top. He knelt on the floor and put his arms on the edge of my bed in a similar position he was in before he raped me. He sat there for a minute silently looking away from me as though he was contemplating his next move. I wasn't sure what he was doing so I sat up from the laying position I was in. I was scared, broken, damaged, nauseous, and felt disconnected from my worthless, objectified, physical self. *Now that he got what he wanted, what is he going to do next? Is he silent because he is planning something? Is he contemplating killing me?*

He noticed my body shaking and gave me a small hug. *Gross. Get the fuck off me,* I thought. He seemed concerned that I was scared out of my mind and continued to hug me. *What the hell is happening?* He said, "Sorry. I'm sorry. If it's any consolation, it felt so fucking good." *No, you asshole. It is not a consolation.*

But he still wasn't leaving. His body language reminded me of someone who was showing regret. How could this be, when in my opinion, he was probably a sociopath? And then it struck me. Maybe it was regret for what he was about to do? I quickly needed to rationalize with this monster. I had to appeal to any small shred of humanity there was left in him. I had to take back my power and show him I was a whole, smart, worthy human being. I needed him to see I had a good heart and soul, and a family I loved dearly. I was not an object.

I finally asked, "Are you okay?" I needed to figure out what was going on in his head and what he was planning to do.

He laughed a little and asked, "Don't tell me you're getting Stockholm syndrome?"

I replied, "I don't know what that is." He explained it was when the person being kidnapped falls in love with the kidnapper. He was right about one thing; I was kidnapped. I was a prisoner, a hostage, in my own home.

"No. You just don't seem okay. But you're clever, I didn't know what that was," I tried to connect with him.

This situation isn't something they prepare you for in high school. It isn't something they prepare you for in college. I was not prepared for any part of being held against my will in my own home and being raped. All I knew of situations like mine came from what I had seen in movies. I remembered bits and pieces of how characters had gotten out of a dangerous situation.

I continued, "You know, Anne Frank said, 'I still believe people are good at heart'," *you fucking psycho.*

When I was young, I believed what Anne Frank had said. I drew the quote on a piece of notebook paper and shaded the entire page with pencil around the quote. I lined the quote with glow-in-the-dark gel and hung it up on my bedroom door so I could read it even after the lights were out. I gave people the benefit of the doubt, just like my mom. What was happening to me during those early morning hours was not processing like real-life. It felt like a nightmare. It felt like a horror movie. I was now experiencing impending doom, preparing for him to attempt to kill me now that he got what he wanted.

The man grabbed my hand with his bare right hand. The sliver of orange glow from the streetlight across the road was providing enough light through my closed curtains for me to see his hand was white. Narrowing it down... this man was Caucasian. It was also rough, like a working man's hand. He put his head covered with the mask on my right shoulder when I noticed his small black phone on my bed. I saw a small white light on the front of the phone blinking. I pointed out, "You have a message." Who the hell gets a text message at that hour of the morning? Was that why his phone was blinking?

"You gotta stop noticing shit." He slipped his phone into the pocket of his black sweatpants. This snapped him back into anger.

He stood and asked, "What are you going to do when I leave?"

"Lie in bed with my son," I replied, as it was indisputably the only thing in the world I wanted to do.

Right next to my bed was a mahogany-colored wooden

nightstand. It had my lamp, water cup, and three small drawers containing socks, underwear, and miscellaneous things.

The man opened the top drawer of my nightstand and started digging around. I don't know what led him to do this, but he joked about what he might find. He asked if he would find sex toys and dildos. While he was joking, he found the two loaded gun clips Cody had left for me. He set them on the nightstand and asked with urgency, "Where are the guns?"

The tone of his voice scared the hell out of me. I hadn't gone for them to defend myself because the guns were nowhere near the clips. He suddenly felt under my mattress and under my pillow where I wished I had loaded guns. Instead, my guns were not loaded, and nowhere near my pillow. He dug through the rest of my drawers. "Where are they?" he demanded. He seemed utterly manic.

Cooperate. I've made it this far.

I told him they were in the closet. What other choice did I have? He had his own loaded gun, why would having two more be any different? I should have said I didn't know where they were. I should have said Cody had them, but that probably would have pissed him off even more. He stood up and commanded, "Turn over. Face down," in a voice that I prayed wouldn't wake James.

I complied.

He went over to the closet and opened the doors, "Where are they?"

"On the top shelf," I said.

He pulled down the black gun case from my top shelf and asked, "Is this yours?"

"No. My ex-husband left them here," I explained. Cody had left them for me in case I ever needed them. Unfortunately, that didn't work out according to plan.

He mentioned my ex-husband and I had a weird relationship since we were obviously still close. And it was true, I did still love Cody.

He found the second pistol and now had three guns with three sets of ammo. All I had was hope I would live to see tomorrow to hear my little boy's heartbeat. It was the only thing that kept me fighting this silent fight. Years later I would understand that I was David and he was Goliath.

Not knowing what he was doing left me feeling terrified; I was still face down with my back to him. I heard his voice move from a standing position to a crouching position. He opened the gun case and asked, "So if I kill you with this gun, they'll think it was your ex-husband?"

I knew it. Here we go. I'm going to die. The feeling of impending death was killing me inside, as ironic as it sounds.

I quietly but hysterically begged him, "No. He's in Pennsylvania working. There is proof of that! He's not even in this state. *My* handprints are on those guns. Please, please don't."

"Is he still in the picture? Your son's dad?" I didn't understand how he was so calm when I was so hysterical.

"He doesn't live with me," I managed to reply.

"What does he do for a living?" he asked; I had no idea why he cared but I told him anyway.

Then I heard a gun being manipulated. I was certain he was loading and racking it to shoot me with Cody's gun.

I begged again, "Please, please don't kill me. Please!"

Surprisingly, his voice was calm as he explained, "Oh. I suppose I'm scaring the shit out of you. I'm just unloading the magazine."

Fucking asshole.

He threw the parts in my laundry basket. They landed at the bottom with a thud, and he said, "This works better if you have laundry in your laundry basket. Quit being so damn clean." He said it like he had done this before, causing me to believe this wasn't his first crime.

"Do you have an iPod or a speaker? Something to play music?" he questioned, completely changing subjects.

"There's an iPad in the bathroom on the counter. There's a speaker by the staircase."

"Don't move," he demanded. He knew how scared I was and seemed to enjoy watching my fear grow as the time passed. He trusted that fear enough to leave the bedroom.

He came back to the hallway at the entryway of my door telling me how he was going to disable my phone and iPad so I couldn't make calls. I didn't know at what point he took my phone from my bedside stand. He must have taken it right away. He expressed frustration that he wouldn't be able to use the Bluetooth JBL speaker with my iPad if it was disabled.

"Do you have any other phones or devices? Anything?" he asked.

"I have an Apple Watch in the hallway closet," I replied. He wanted to be sure everything was disabled so I couldn't make any phone calls.

I turned my head and saw him standing near the dresser. He had the hallway light on allowing me to see a silhouette of his nose. It was slightly larger than average size, lacking any bump or flip at the end. I memorized it.

He came to the bed and put the speaker on my pillow above my head and told me to try to get it to work. I was pressing the buttons and looking at my iPad, but the speaker wasn't connecting. He walked back into the hallway and as he did music started blaring from the JBL speaker. The song that came on was *I'm Sexy and I Know It* by LMFAO. Turns out, it wasn't connecting to the iPad because the speaker was connected to my phone.

James is going to wake up!

I urgently turned the volume down. My heart raced. *Hurry, hurry! Please, God. Please help him stay asleep!*

I listened intently to hear if any noise would come from James's room. I heard nothing.

To this day, I can't listen to that dreadful song. If I hear it, I'm instantly taken back to that moment. The man gave up on trying to get the speaker to work so he put the iPad on my pillow and said, "Don't move. Let it play through at least seven songs. After seven songs, I'll be outta here." He paused, "What are you going to do when I leave?"

"I'm going to lay in bed with my son," I repeated.

It was around this time when he was leaving my room that I asked him to please leave my son alone and stay out of his bedroom.

He replied, **"I am a rapist, not a monster."**

I will never forget that.

When I didn't reply to his comment, he continued, "That was supposed to be a joke," and the bedroom door closed behind him with country music playing on Pandora.

I was alone. It was time to do some serious planning. *How am I going to save my son? How am I going to get us out of here?* I listened as hard as I could to be sure he wasn't going into James's room.

I never heard another door open other than my own when he came in every few minutes to check on me. He would open the door, notice me in the same position he left me in, say, "Good," and leave again. He spent a notable amount of time in my house but not in my bedroom. I had no idea what he was doing but my mind contemplated a variety of scenarios. *Is he planting cameras? Is he stealing everything? Is he destroying my house? Is he looking for something in particular?*

After about four songs he came back in and asked again, "What are you going to do when I leave?"

I said, "I'm going to the bathroom, then I'm going to lay in bed with my son."

He asked if I wanted to go now and I said, "No, I'll wait until you leave."

"Just go now," he insisted. So I stood up with only my blue Volcom shirt on and nothing else. I tip-toed my way into the bathroom. He demanded I keep the door open. I sat down in the light of my bathroom and tried to pee while he watched. I kept my head down and faced forward. My bladder was full, but I couldn't do it.

I stood up and said, "I can't. I'm pee shy."

He allowed me to shut the door but warned me not to do anything stupid.

I shut the door and sat down again. I didn't dare lock it. I was finally able to pee, even as I saw his flashlight shine at my feet from under the door. I had wished I had a gun stashed in there, or a knife, or a panic button to an alarm system. But I didn't. I had nothing. All I had was the slightest bit of privacy as I was going to the bathroom after being raped twice by this monster.

When I finished, I wiped myself. There would still be plenty of evidence inside my body, all over my skin, my sheets, and plenty of other places. As soon as I was done in the bathroom, I opened the door and was blinded by his flashlight shining directly into my face. He seemed to have been in a crouching position at the end of my hallway, watching me from under the door I assumed. Looking in his direction was a huge mistake. I stood in the doorway and asked if I should go back to the bedroom and he yelled, "Go!"

I went back to my room and assumed the position I was in prior to getting up. I laid on my stomach but this time I covered myself up with my gray comforter. He followed me into the room, threw the covers off me, forcefully pulled my shirt up from covering my bare body and grabbed my bare hips. He pulled them up with force and aggressively raped me again. I felt rage with every thrust, and anger with every threat. Any regret he once had earlier was completely gone. He threatened me as he raped me and I sobbed with fear, each additional threat feeding the hopelessness I felt. I was completely defeated and lacking any ounce of control.

He pushed me down. My face landed on the pillow and I was facing the window. My arms were up by my side, by my tear-soaked face. He put his right arm on my back and his face came close to mine. I was a rag doll, an object, a lifeless body once again. I saw silver on the two-toned gun next to my left eye. He was inches from me when he threatened, "You're *not* going to call the cops. You're *not* going to tell anyone."

He moved back down my body, in between my legs. His hand was on my left thigh when suddenly he lifted my hips again and put his face on my bare body and kissed my naked-ness in a way that made me feel disgusted, exposed, and beyond violated. I wanted to scream; I wanted to cry; I wanted to turn around and punch him in the face, but there was nothing I could do without waking up James.

When his head was between my legs, I saw a flash of light as I faced my headboard. I wondered if it was his flashlight or a phone light. *Did he take a picture?*

After the third time I was raped, he threatened me again, "I'd hate to have to come back for you. I'd hate to have to go to your son's school and kill him. I will be watching you. I know how to get into your house."

I told him again I would rather be alive with my son than tell anyone about this.

The man left my bedroom once again after turning music on. As I lie in bed, feeling more defeated than I would have dreamed possible, I hoped to God I would finally hear him leave... but I didn't. I had disassociated from my body, but my mind was one hundred percent intact. I *could not* and *would not* give up for my son. As awful and revengeful as I felt, I still would have done anything to ensure my little man's safety.

I felt like my body was physically unable to move. I suddenly weighed 500 lbs. I had no control over my physical self and the defeat I felt before had multiplied by a million. I heard noises throughout my house, but I couldn't figure out what he was doing out there. Since I couldn't move, all I could do was try to hear any noise he made through the music.

I froze as I heard his footsteps outside my door. I waited for him to open it, wondering if he was coming back to rape me a fourth time. My stomach churned as I heard what sounded like his gun dragging across my wooden bedroom door. He was antagonizing me, taunting me, and continuously instilling fear into me, waiting for me to make one wrong move.

When he came back again, he put his knee on my bed, leaned near my head and said in a short, somber tone, "I'm sorry for this whole night. Do you want to go lay with your son?"

"Yes," I replied

"Go," he offered, but continued with, "You know when I leave, I will be outside so I wouldn't recommend going out his window."

"It is the second story; I am not going to go out the window." *Unfortunately.*

With no hesitation, I tiptoed to my son's room without looking directly at the man. I opened the door and closed it quietly behind me hoping I wouldn't wake James. I crawled in bed with my sleeping little boy, but I was shaking so intensely that he woke up a little. I tried to control my breathing, but it was damn-near impossible. I didn't lock the door. I thought it would make him angry and I didn't want him to think we were up to anything he wouldn't approve of.

I was thankful he hadn't been in my son's room; he hadn't touched the life that meant more to me than my own. He came to the door and said deeply, "Hey. Are you still in there?" I sat up and let him know I was. This seemed to satisfy him enough to step away again.

James stirred and said, "I want to go to Daddy's house." He heard the man's voice and thought it was Cody.

I tried to keep him calm and whispered, "Honey, that isn't Daddy. It's okay, buddy. It's not time to wake up yet."

He wasn't fully awake at this point, and I was able to snuggle him back to sleep. I heard the sink in the bathroom running, turning on and off intermittently. Then I heard the tub running for a long period of time. I heard the man stomp downstairs to the basement and wondered what he could possibly be doing down there.

A short while later the man came back to make sure we were there. The final time he came to the door he asked, "Hey. Are you awake? Come to the door." *He thought I'd be able to fall asleep after this!*

"Yes, yes," I got up immediately and went to the door so I wouldn't have to talk over my son's sleeping body.

"I'm going to set a timer on your iPad. When the timer goes off, I'll be outta here." The door was cracked open as he was talking.

"Mommy, Mommy. Who is here?" James asked as he crawled out of bed and made his way to the door.

"No, honey, go back to bed. It's okay, bud," I said as I shut the door quietly on the man. I didn't stop to make sure he was done talking to me. I didn't want to risk any contact or communication between him and my son.

"Mommy, who is here? Why is the shower on?" James asked.

I picked him up and carried him back to bed. I explained that a worker-man was there to fix our shower. As usual, for any inquisitive three-year-old, this led to many more questions. "Why is the man here? Why is the shower broken? Can we go out there? Can we turn on the light?"

He was wide awake at this point so I told him we could play with toys in his bed, but we couldn't turn on the bedroom light or leave the room. Hours must have passed since I first woke up at 1:27 a.m. Maybe it was time for James to wake up... maybe the man let me go in his room just in time before James would have come out on his own. I had no idea what time it was.

After a few moments of playing, James whined, "Mommy, I have a tummy-ache. It hurts really bad."

"What's wrong, peanut?" I asked.

"I have to go potty," he said. *Oh, honey...*

"Okay, buddy. Okay." I looked around my son's room. *Improvise, Danielle. Think.*

I grabbed my son's little garbage can with cute monkeys on the side. I dumped it out into the corner of his room as he crawled out of bed. I was kneeling on the carpet as I put the empty garbage can in front of him. I wrapped my arm around his little three-year-old body and looked at him with tears welling in my eyes and said, "Sweetie, Santa is watching you, and he wants you to be a really good boy for Mommy. Okay? I need you to go potty in your garbage can. The worker-man is fixing our shower, so we can't go into the bathroom. The potty might not be working."

"But why?" he questioned, as any three-year-old would.

"I'm not sure, honey," I replied as he was pulling down his shorts and his *Paw Patrol* underwear.

He looked at me with those innocent eyes and said, "Okay, Mommy."

Heart. Shattered. But we're alive. I will keep you safe, my sweet boy.

He was able to pee into his garbage can. When he finished, he pulled up his underwear and shorts and I moved the garbage can aside. We crawled back into bed and continued to play quietly until I heard the man again.

I heard his heavy boots run down the steps and into my

garage. I heard the door open. He was leaving out my garage. *Now he knows what I drive.* All I heard now was the iPad playing country music. A short amount of time later, the iPad alarm went off. I let it sound for a little bit to be sure I didn't hear the man come back.

Pulling together my nerves, I hesitantly walked to the door and cracked it open. The hallway light was on and there was no sign of the man. On the carpet outside James' bedroom was my iPad with the alarm going off next to my cell phone. I quickly grabbed the iPad, the source of the noise, but left my cell phone. I didn't touch my phone. I shut off the alarm and got back in bed with my son. We pulled up Netflix and watched Jim Carrey in *The Grinch*. My son was making his usual early morning conversation while I pretended to watch the movie. But all I could do was listen for the man. I no longer heard him.

6:15 a.m.

My iPad showed nearly five hours from the last time I had looked at a clock.

5

I STILL HAD THE STEAK KNIFE IN MY SLEEVE WHEN A POLICE officer came into the women's bathroom at Mike's Grocery Store. "I'm Officer Renee Hewitt. Can you tell me what happened?"

I felt some relief seeing a police officer with us. Without saying anything, I pulled the knife from my sleeve and gave it to her. The words in my head were in an intense game of pinball, bouncing around trying to find a way out. I finally managed to say through fearful hesitation, tears, and shame, "A man broke into my house. He raped me. He said he would kill us if I told anyone."

I wished she had come with a team of police officers. I knew the rapist was taller than Officer Hewitt and if he was in the grocery store watching us, he could have easily taken her out leaving us with no protection.

"We'll need to go to the station," she told my mom.

But my mom's motherly instincts kicked in and she said, "No. She needs to go to the emergency room. She needs to be evaluated."

Officer Hewitt made a phone call to her chief and while she

was on the phone, my mom went out to the car to talk to my dad. By the time Officer Hewitt was off the phone, my mom returned to the bathroom.

"Are you ready?" Officer Hewitt asked. *Okay Danielle, think. What am I supposed to say now? How do I do this thing called life? I thought it was over.* "Yes," I said. I didn't want to leave the bathroom, fearful he was out there waiting for us, but I knew we had to. I wanted to continue to move away from this nightmare.

Officer Hewitt escorted us through the store and outside. *No sign of him...*

"Do you want to ride with me or ride with your mom?" she asked. I hesitated. Did I want to be with an officer who was armed and trained to defend?

"I'll ride with my parents. I need to stay with my son," I decided.

I strapped James into the car seat my mom kept in her car and sat in the seat next to him. My mom climbed in the driver's side and my dad was silently sitting in the front passenger seat. He was a man of few words, but I knew he was glad I was okay.

I felt numb and broken, like a zombie wandering out in the fog wondering what my purpose was and what I was supposed to do next. All I could do was lay quietly with my head on my son's lap.

My aunt Lisa met us outside of the ER to get James. My mom had called her on our way to town. When I saw her, I instantly began crying. Here was my son's ticket to safety, to a place where he wouldn't have to hear or see what was about to happen—interrogations while nurses examined my entire body and swabbed me for DNA.

My aunt opened the car door to get my son and I reached across and gave her a big hug. I was grateful to be alive and to be able to hug her, feeling her blonde silky hair on my tear-stained face.

"It's okay, honey. It's okay. You can go with Auntie Lisa.

You'll be with the big dogs and they'll keep you safe. Mommy will be there as soon as I can. I love you!" I hugged my son so tight in that moment. I didn't want to let go.

"Okay, Mommy. I love you," he said. Without hesitation, he went with my aunt. When they walked to her car, my heart was breaking with every step she took. Further and further away he was from me, but closer to safety and away from this nightmare.

We were greeted at the door of the ER where I was offered a wheelchair. I declined. I had my mom on one side of me and Officer Hewitt on the other.

"Danielle Louise Leukam," I told the receptionist when she asked for my name. They knew I was coming and immediately escorted us into a quiet room in a back wing. I was greeted by two SANE nurses, Mayo Clinic's Sexual Assault Nurse Examiners, specifically trained to perform rape kits on sexual assault survivors. I was also greeted by an Olmsted County Victim's Advocate. I was still afraid, but I kept reminding myself I was with Officer Hewitt and was in the safest place I could be.

"Here's a gown for you to change into. Please put your shirt and underwear into this bag. We'll also need you to pee in this cup," one of the nurses said. I went into the bathroom and stood there for a moment. *What is happening?* Shock was trying to take over but I had to stay alert and oriented, and remind myself why I was in the ER. I placed my shirt and underwear into the bag and put on the robe.

I cracked open the door, "Um... can I wipe after I pee in the cup?"

"Oh, yes. We will still be able to find evidence. Don't worry," the lead SANE nurse said. Then I remembered I'd gotten sick before James and I left the house, so it was too late anyway. Her kindness was overwhelming but welcomed after a morning of terror.

After the small stuff was accomplished (insurance paperwork and updating hospital records), I had to tell the SANE nurses and Officer Hewitt what happened. The entire story. It was a five-hour long event compacted into twenty minutes or so, and it was hard to piece everything together in order. I kept remembering things as they asked questions and had to backtrack to add more details I had suddenly remembered. I was feeling a weird sort of calm at times but a moment later I'd break down, become afraid, then feel a deep rage building in my chest. I sobbed to my mom, "Why me? I don't understand. Why is it always me?"

And it was true. I had been sexually assaulted by someone multiple times prior to separating from my husband. Then I was sexually assaulted three times in the year following our separation. Four different men had touched me when they knew damn well they shouldn't have, without my permission. *Why the hell do they see a giant target on my forehead? What am I missing? Is it because I'm Minnesota-Nice all of the time? Am I too nice?*

My mom replied in the warmest embrace, "I don't know, honey. But let's not try to figure it out right now."

I'd been treated like an object before, but this was the first time I had been raped. And I would make for damn sure it would be the last.

I finally felt safe enough to turn on my phone. If he was able to track me with my phone, at least I was in a hospital with an officer. I received a couple of messages in which I briefly replied.

One was from my neighbor Kaila. She asked, *Is everything okay??*

There must have been cops at my house, so I replied. *No. Keep your doors and windows locked.* Then my phone was taken as evidence. I hadn't even gotten the chance to message Brian, the man I had been seeing for the last couple of months.

"I want to make sure you know everything we're going to be doing before we do it. Please tell me to stop at any point you don't feel comfortable. Do you have any questions?" the nurse asked.

"No," I said, knowing what was going to happen, having learned the basics in nursing school.

She started to explain the process and asked, "Do you feel comfortable proceeding with this portion of the examination?"

"Yes," *I provided consent.* It felt good to be asked.

I had my neck swabbed where he kissed, both on the right side and the left. I had my body checked for DNA under a black light; they would also be able to see where bruises may form with this light. They checked for and documented marks on my body and noted every zip tie mark on my wrists. This part seemed to take a while since I had multiple deep marks from every time I tried to adjust my wrists. The marks were still easily visible even after hours of having the zip ties off.

I had to have a full body and vaginal exam. The most private parts of my body were examined by both nurses and photographed by a female photographer. She also took photos of my wrists and a picture of my face.

WHILE SHE WAS TAKING pictures up close and personal, my mom stepped out to call Cody, and my boss, Jenny. Cody was the first person I wanted her to call. Despite being in the middle of a divorce, I still loved Cody and trusted him deeply. I knew he would want to know what happened and it was important to keep him in the loop, especially considering James's life was threatened.

Cody was at work in Pennsylvania when Mom called. When she told him what happened, he was instantly furious.

He got a ride back to where he was staying to pack his bags and hop on the first flight back to Minnesota.

When Mom returned, she said, "Cody is switching his flight so he can come home tonight. He'll be on the first flight he can get." I later found out he spent $800 on a ticket to come home. This was one of the reasons I had loved Cody profoundly, and still do, as my son's father.

Tears streamed down my face as I said, "Okay," but I couldn't pinpoint what tears they were. Relief that he would keep us safe? Guilt? Shame?

I HAD TAKEN A PREGNANCY TEST. I had taken a Plan B pill. I had blood drawn. I had taken multiple antibiotics to treat sexually transmitted infections. And I had to expose my entire body to multiple people. I was experiencing many things I never knew I would have to experience in my lifetime.

"Since you don't know the person who raped you, we're going to offer you to be treated for HIV. Is this something you'd like to move forward with? We would refer you to an Infectious Disease provider."

What...?!

I hadn't thought about that. It was a shock to try to process, but I did what I had to do.

"Yes, please."

The nurses gave me a long-sleeve pink T-shirt, a new pair of underwear, and a bag with bathroom essentials: toothpaste, toothbrush, shampoo, conditioner, and soap. They knew I wouldn't be going home. These items that had been prepared for these kinds of situations and to this day, I still have the pink shirt and underwear. The support, kindness, and care I received in the ER gave me hope.

After hearing the details of the attack and the threats made against James, Officer Hewitt and the SANE nurses said, "That's what they *all* say." They all threaten to kill you. What was heart-breaking to me about this was they said *all*. *They all*. Multiple rapists, multiple victims, multiple women and men who have gone through the same thing as me.

The lead SANE nurse said, "You saved your life. You saved your son's life. You are so clever for the things you said to him. It was so smart of you—you were thinking so clearly. You truly saved your lives." These words gave me hope for being able to overcome the rest of what this nightmare would bring. A new feeling overcame me in that moment. It was powerful and uplifting, and the only words I could put to the feeling were: *I survived.*

6

Hours after being dismissed from the ER, my mom asked if I was hungry. *No.* "Sure," I gave in. It seemed like the right thing to do. I was nervous to go in public, but a warm bowl of soup was the only thing that sounded appetizing. I was in zombie mode, so I simply went along with whatever was offered to me.

We went to Panera near the hospital. I decided on comfort food: half of a sandwich and a cup of tomato soup. I hadn't eaten anything since the day prior, with the exception of a small amount of chicken noodle soup in the ER to help with some of the medications I had taken. I looked at everyone in Panera, particularly the males. Could they tell I was nervous? Did they know what happened? Could they see it in my face? I tried to play cool and pretend like I wasn't dying inside.

I was using my mom's phone to chat with a few select loved ones, including Cody and Jenny since my phone was now evidence. I was happy to be breathing and relieved to be alive. I was comforted a little with the warm soup but I was eager to get to my aunt's house—the safe place where my son and two big dogs, one of which was a protective German Shepherd named Huck, were waiting for me.

. . .

AFTER GETTING to my aunt's house I took a bath. A long, hot bath in which I scrubbed away the evidence, the hurt, and the disgust I felt. I tried, anyway. I scrubbed off any part of the rapist that could have possibly been left on me.

Next to the tub lay my long-sleeved pink shirt and underwear from the ER. The reality of the situation began to kick in. Everything was so up in the air: my house, my car, my work, my safety, James's safety. My whole life as I knew it was completely turned upside down. I would never sleep in my house again. He would surely come back for me. I'd never again sleep in my beautiful bedroom Cody had painted or wake up to see the photos of James hanging on the wall. I'd never hear James sneak into that bedroom, grab my gray comforter that was now in evidence, and watch him crawl his little body up onto my bed. I'd never watch the sunrise out my back patio as I enjoyed coffee on the deck. Instead, I would live at my aunt's house and occasionally stay at my parents' house for the next month and a half.

My mind kept going back to him saying, "I've been waiting for years to be in this position." *Who are you? What kind of monster have I allowed in my life that could do such a thing to us?*

I wished I could rewind time to load a gun and put it under my pillow. I wished I would have double and triple checked the door locks *and* the windows. But despite what I could have done differently, he still would have found a way in. A gun was already pointed at my head before I would have had time to grab my own.

I wished I had gone to the skating rink with my aunt and her family. Maybe then I would have had a glass of wine in the hot tub at her house and we would have spent the night. Maybe if my roommate hadn't moved out two months earlier, if my dog Marley hadn't died two months earlier, if I hadn't been going through a divorce, I wouldn't have been alone. Maybe he wouldn't have come. Maybe Marley would have barked at him. Maybe seeing Cody in bed next to me would have scared him away. Maybe.

What if my son couldn't sleep and had come in my room to crawl into bed with me? What if the man's finger had pulled a little too hard while it was on the trigger of the gun pointed at my head? What if he had put four pounds of pressure on that trigger, just enough to make it fire? What if I hadn't cooperated with his commands? What if he didn't listen when I told him to not drug me? What if I was meant to die?

I can't tell you to this day why I told him what Anne Frank said. Maybe I was saying it for my own sake. Maybe I was trying to convince him that he could still be a good person. Truthfully, I am not entirely sure I agree with Anne Frank anymore. I sure as hell didn't at that moment.

Had the other sexual assault and harassment situations since separating from Cody lead up to this? Did I deserve this? Is that why I was cooperative? Had those incidents molded my mind to expect this is the way men treat me? Why does it feel like all of those situations led up to that morning? *Why me? Why does this happen to me?*

That morning had been the perfect storm for this rapist. I was sleeping soundly alone in bed with no dog, no roommate, no security system, and no man. It's like he knew.

THE NEXT FEW days were a blur. I was in shock, making my way through time like I was walking through a burning cornfield maze with smoke barreling in all around me as the flames grew higher. I kept my head down and put one foot in front of the other, trying to carry on.

I realized within those first few days I couldn't wear tight shirts. I only felt comfortable in loose, long sleeve tops but only had a couple that my aunt lent me along with the shirt from the ER. The rest of my clothes remained at home—in the crime scene.

Cody arrived back in Minnesota late in the evening of the eighteenth and sent my mom a text as soon as his plane landed, *I'll come see her and James tomorrow. Thank you for taking care of them.*

He came to my aunt's house the next morning and I was emotional upon seeing him. I was grateful he was a good man and selfishly wanted him around because he made me feel safe. "Thank you so much," I cried. "Thank you for coming."

Cody and I went up to my temporary room at my aunt's house and I told him the details of what happened. I wanted him to know just in case something happened to me. Then someone else would know the story and would be able to tell it on my behalf. I was also hoping something within the story would help us narrow down a suspect list.

"My mom said she would have James with her for a few days while we figure things out," Cody told me.

"Thank you. Thank her for me. It's probably for the best. It's not safe down here. I don't know when we will ever be safe."

I was numb. I can't say I would have been a great mom in the week following the assault considering the zombie-like state I was in. I did *not* want to be away from my son, but he needed to be surrounded by love, laughter, family, and happiness.

I WENT to a doctor appointment to meet with an Infectious Disease provider. They prescribed me HIV prophylaxis medications and Zofran to take as needed for nausea, knowing that's a common side effect. She told me they would have to check my blood to make sure my body was tolerating the medications. I later learned from "Dr. Google" they could cause kidney and liver issues. *Hmm, HIV or potential kidney failure? I guess potential kidney failure it is...*

Rather than having to wait for the medications at the pharmacy, my aunt took me back to her house. My uncle generously offered to pick them up for me when they were ready. I was sitting on the couch when he walked in. He didn't want to say anything, I could tell, but something was off.

"Thank you so much for picking those up for me. How much did they cost?" I asked.

He hesitated. "$760," he replied, trying to be honest but not make me feel bad at the same time. *What?*

"Oh my God," I said.

My aunt chimed in, "Don't worry about it, honey."

"I will talk with the Victim's Advocate from Winona County to see if I can get reimbursed. I'm so sorry. Thank you so much for picking them up." I didn't have that kind of money; I couldn't offer to repay him out of my own funds.

THERE WAS a press release on November 20, 2018:

ST. CHARLES, Minn. (FOX 47) – St. Charles Police and the Winona County Sheriff's Department are investigating and armed home invasion and assault.

The invasion happened early Sunday morning in St. Charles.

Investigators said they believe the crime was targeted.

The suspect is described as a 6' tall white male with average build who appears to be in his 30s.

St. Charles Police Department said that while they do believe it was a targeted crime, they want to remind the public to lock their doors and windows and be aware of their surroundings.

Anyone with information is urged to contact St. Charles Police Department.

IT WAS good to see the story was being covered because maybe someone would pipe up with more information. At the same time, I was terrified because if he saw the article, he would know the authorities were aware of the situation. It seemed likely to me he was from the area and surely would discover the news. I needed to hide from the world so he, whoever he was, couldn't find me.

I Googled the story and one article turned into multiple articles ranging from Winona County to Olmsted County to Duluth, the Twin Cities, and all the way out to northwest Minnesota. It was a reality check for me. Not only did my family know, *Minnesota* knew.

What will they think? Will they believe me? Will they think he's a monster too? I hoped it inspired families to get security systems and be sure *all* their doors and windows were locked.

My MOM HAD TAKEN three days off work to be with me. Sometime that first week, she drove me to the clinic where I had planned to meet with Jenny at work. When I got to our floor, she and I hugged a hug I will never forget. I couldn't help but to cry hard despite how strong I attempted to be. "I'm so happy to see you! I'm so happy *to be able to* see you!" Jenny had been an angel and a blessing in my life.

"I'm so happy you're okay! Do you need anything? What can I do?" she asked.

"I'm just happy to be here." And by here, I meant alive.

We snuck into a conference room where I logged on to a computer, read through some emails and set my "Out of Office" reply. We shed tears of happiness and sadness and heartbreak. I had somehow escaped zombie mode and was able to feel again. I was grateful to be alive and able to see her beautiful pregnant belly and hear her special laugh.

"How much time do you need off work?" she asked.

I had no idea. I hadn't thought about it. But now all of the things I would need to do were swimming through my mind like dozens of minnows in a pail of water.

"Maybe just the rest of this week?" I hesitantly asked.

My mom and Jenny weren't convinced that I would be well

enough to be able to come back after only one week. We settled on two weeks. I planned to talk to my primary care provider about this to determine how to move forward with work, appointments, and my mental stability. After two weeks, the third week was a week I had already planned to take off of work. I felt awful taking time off; it wasn't easy to replace my position. But at the same time, was I ready to go back? *Absolutely not.* I kept questioning who this monster was, and asked myself, *What if it was someone from work?* In the end, I agreed I needed time to get things in order and to process and heal. Maybe I'd be lucky enough they would find the rapist by the time I had to go back to work. I also needed time to sell my vehicle and buy a new one, apply for my permit to carry, go to doctor appointments, change my address, forward my mail, go to interviews with the investigators, and start to rebuild my entire life.

My aunt was a stay-at-home mom, so I was able to spend quality time with her while I attempted to settle in. It was also nice not having to be alone.

We sat in her hot tub outside one evening and talked about what happened over a bottle of wine. I completed Sober-October a few weeks before this, and throughout the beginning of November I only had a glass of wine here and there. But here I was, drinking every night since the assault.

"So, who do you think it was, Danielle?" my aunt asked.

"I have no idea. I mean, I've been turning people down for dates since separating from Cody. What if it was someone from my high school?" I questioned.

"Do you have any ex-boyfriends it could have been? What about that guy you dated when you were eighteen? The one with the blue hair?"

"Nah, that wasn't his body type. I don't know. I just don't

know! I should get a yearbook to look through. I mean, obviously it was someone who knows where I live. Or maybe someone was stalking me."

I was angry thinking, *Life shouldn't have to be like this—living in fear, afraid to be in public, afraid for my child's life.* We had done nothing wrong. I replayed the night over in my mind envisioning the five hours with each one of the suspects we came up with trying to figure out if they were a match. No one came up as a solid lead.

MY MOM CALLED the Red Cross to make arrangements to notify my sister. The Red Cross contacted the Winona County Investigator working on the case to verify this was a credible situation. Once confirmed, they had my sister's commander in the military and a chaplain notify her. She called my mom afterwards to get more details because they apparently did not say much.

My mom later told me Erin was angry and had the same question I continued to have, "Why her? Why do men do this to her? Why does this happen to her?" I cried when I found out my big sister was able to fly back from Kuwait for a few days. Erin wanted to talk to me on the phone, but I wasn't ready to talk. I wouldn't have been able to hold my composure. I felt gross, broken, violated, and disgusting, and I didn't want to hear any words related to what happened. I didn't want to cry anymore. She later texted my mom asking, *How do I know she is okay? Ask her who our favorite Disney star is. The one with the blonde hair.*

My mom showed me the text, so I took the phone and replied, *Hilary Duff. And fuck Colbie Caillat.* We didn't like Colbie Caillat for some reason. It must have been one of her songs that annoyed us, so we established that our dislike for her was something we had in common. Now that we no longer associate her music with past relationships, she is growing on us. *No offense, Colbie.* After I said this, she knew I was okay. As okay as I could be anyway.

She was set to arrive in town the evening prior to Thanksgiving, the Wednesday following the assault. It would take her almost one full day to get home. I felt bad she had to travel so far alone and think about what happened all by herself, but also grateful I would soon have her by my side.

When Erin finally got there, we embraced in a long, close hug. I felt whole knowing she was with me. My heart hurt, my head hurt, my spirit hurt, but she was my fire. She was my fire while Cody was my oxygen. Those two together brought me back to life.

I felt like I needed to tell her everything that happened. I wanted her to be able to ask me questions, offer advice and opinions, to be my personal bodyguard and investigator, and to think of suspects I hadn't thought of. I wanted her to know, just like with Cody, in case something happened to me and I wouldn't be able to tell the story myself. I was apprehensive about it though and it was extremely hard to find the words. I felt ashamed. Like the whole situation was *my* fault and I had put my son in danger.

When I finally found a starting point, I felt like a robot trying to recite a five-hour movie line-for-line, "So... I went to bed. And I heard a noise at the end of my bed. I thought it was the cats." I spoke quickly in monotone and tried to remember everything. Like with the SANE nurses, I had to backtrack at times because I would get the story out of order and remember bits and pieces as I continued.

When I reached the end of the story, I finished with, "...and mom called 911."

Telling my sister what happened was like filling in my other half, but I'm sure it was hard for her to hear. She was quiet while I spoke and remained calm while we talked about potential suspects.

"Could it have been that one guy who kept asking you out?" she asked. "Who knows where you live?"

"I don't know. I mean, maybe. Not many people know where I live," I replied. I had only been living in my house in St. Charles for a year and a half.

During her travels back to the United States, she did some digging through my friend list on Facebook and Instagram and came up with a few additional names for our suspect list. Since I had immediately deactivated my social media platforms, I didn't have access to, nor did I care to, look through my accounts myself. Erin also brought old yearbooks we had planned to go through.

Erin knew me. She knew the people in my life. She brought a sense of protection, much like Cody did, and it made me feel at home even though I no longer had a home.

MY MOM WANTED to make sure I had everything I needed for living at my aunt's house, so she took me to the grocery store named Hy-Vee to grab snacks and essentials. I was glued to her side while we walked around the store. My beautiful mother was taller than me, strong, and brave, yet kind and compassionate. I felt safe with her despite the fact that every man in the store was a suspect.

It was in the cracker aisle where things became more intense. My mom and I were choosing crackers to bring to my aunt's house for Thanksgiving when a man came near us and said, "Excuse me, you ladies seem to know a lot about crackers. What would you recommend with a salmon Thanksgiving dinner?"

I had an internal panic attack. I looked at the man's nose and hands. I tucked myself behind my mom towards the shelves. *Is this him? Does he know we're out and about? Did he follow us? Who asks random women about crackers with a salmon dinner!?*

My mom politely answered his questions and he finally walked away satisfied with our recommendations. I didn't say a word. My mom replied to me as if I had expressed my internal concerns verbally, "I know, honey. I'm thinking the same thing as you."

"I was looking at his hands," I managed to whisper.

THURSDAY CAME AND WENT; it happened to be Thanksgiving. I was still a zombie. It did not feel like a holiday despite the family getting together as we normally do, eating turkey, cranberries, and pumpkin pie. My son was with Cody and his family up north, still in a safe place far away from our former home. I didn't know what to say or how to act. I didn't want to talk nor fake being okay, so I spent most of the afternoon coloring in an adult coloring book. Staying focused on coloring helped to pass the time and keep my mind occupied without having to process or talk.

As the fog in my head subsided, I began to process in real-time. One of the first things I had to do was get a computer. I didn't care how much it would cost me; I had to write. Black Friday came and Erin and I drove to Best Buy. There was a sale on a decent computer, but an employee said they had sold out of it earlier in the day. Despite this information, Erin still dug around on the shelves and happened to find it. It was the last one.

I knew I had to lay out everything that happened that morning in writing. To process? To figure out why it happened? To comprehend? To figure out who did it? So I wouldn't forget? It was all of the above, really. I wanted every detail in writing while it was fresh in my mind to tell investigators, a judge, a jury, and maybe someday the man's wife... But also so I could tell the world.

I had eleven pages in a Word document typed up within a day. I was journaling and reflecting, processing the trauma. Eventually the words came out in paragraph form, then chapters, and it was incredibly therapeutic.

ANOTHER THING I had to consider that first week was my vehicle. My SUV sat parked in Mike's Grocery Store parking lot for multiple days until my family was able to move it for me. Since the man left through my garage, he obviously knew what I drove. I had to sell it so he couldn't find me. It was a 2011 black Ford Escape, a perfect single-mom vehicle. I didn't want to sell it; I had planned to drive it until it died. It had 172,000 miles and had been exceptionally reliable. But there was no way in hell I would drive it again. I was frugal and didn't want to buy a new vehicle, until now.

"What am I going to do? I can't drive it. The guy went out of my garage. He'll be able to find me if I'm in the same vehicle," I asked my family. Cody found someone to sell it for me, the owner of an auto-body shop in Eyota, so my sister and I spent an hour detailing it in preparation to sell.

"Do you want to use my Escape when I go back to Kuwait next week?" she offered. Unfortunately, her Escape was nearly the same as mine. My gut told me it wasn't a good idea.

"Thanks, Sissy. I don't think I should drive something that looks the same as mine though. Cody said he could sell it. I'll look at getting something different."

IN THE WEEK FOLLOWING THANKSGIVING, I stayed with Erin in the Twin Cities for a day. We spent hours car shopping. We test drove a black Mazda CX-5. You know, another perfect mom car.

I could travel with my future German Shepherd guard dog I hoped to get, and I could fit golf clubs in the back.

When we went back to the Rochester area, we found another Mazda to test drive. I liked it, but I certainly didn't fall in love. The Mazda drove nice and it was practical, but I didn't feel like being practical. I had a bucket list to attend to now. Surviving a gun pointed at my head, being held hostage, raped three times and saving my son, made me finally want to start living.

"What do you have for cars that are all-wheel drive?" I questioned.

And that's when I found the "race car," as my son would come to call it, that I fell in love with. When I got behind the wheel of the black 2017 Dodge Charger, I knew this one was the one. Adrenaline coursed through my veins and a glimpse of happiness crept into my soul. I was feeling a bit reckless, but it was all-wheel drive and would do well in the snowy winters of Minnesota. It had been my dream car (second to a Challenger) in the past and it was certainly fast enough to get away from anyone who might try to chase me.

I bought the car.

When I started driving myself around again, I made sure to change my routes and take multiple turns. Even though the car was different from the Escape, I still took precaution while out and about. I had to be fine on my own. I had to be smart.

CODY HAD to leave to go back to work on the road after being in Minnesota for a week. I whole-heartedly did not want him to leave. I didn't want to have to say goodbye nor watch James have to say goodbye to his daddy again.

He knelt beside James with his big mechanic's hands wrapped around those three-year-old fingers and said, "I'll be back in three weeks, buddy."

"Daddy, I don't want you to go. Please stay here, Daddy." I was silently hysterical watching James cry and beg his dad to not leave. I cried because my son was sad but I also cried because I didn't want him to leave either. It felt like half of my heart was walking out the door, flying back to Pennsylvania.

"This is the last time I'm leaving, buddy. I'll be home before you know it then after that, I'm not going to leave anymore. It'll be okay. Mommy will take good care of you." Cody decided he would give up his time on the road and this would be his last stretch before coming back to work locally. I was more than grateful for this huge change. It was time for James to have his dad around more than one week a month. I wanted James to be done crying; I wanted to be done crying.

7

MOM AND I DROVE TO THE WOMEN'S RESOURCE CENTER IN Winona, Minnesota for an interview. It was here that I met Investigator Mark Dungy. He seemed kind, but ready to get down to business.

I also officially met Diana, my Victim's Advocate from Winona County. What I liked most about her was how much my mom liked her. She made my mom feel like I was being taken care of, and she presented with years of experience and competence in her role. She offered to sit with me in the interview where I would have to relive the worst morning of my life; I accepted her offer.

Investigator Dungy brought me into the interview room with the advocate by my side. In the room were two leather chairs, fancy carpet, and a rug. It was made to feel like a place to chat rather than an interrogation room. What gave it away were the three cameras set up throughout the room and the window disguised as a mirror. I knew the room behind that mirror housed additional people who were going to be watching me relive those five hours of horror.

"I woke up because I heard a noise at the end of my bed," I started.

I was trying to ignore the cameras and the unknown people on the other side of the glass. Investigator Dungy was thorough with his questions and seemed to care about my feelings throughout the interview. He was experienced and sincere, and I felt comfortable talking with him, regardless of having an advocate next to me.

We took a short break and when I went back into the interview room Dungy said, "We'll need to go back to a couple of parts to collect more details."

It was like recalling scenes from a five-hour movie. The only way I could tell the details of what happened was as if it had happened to someone else. During our second break, I got some water, used the restroom, and checked in with my mom.

"She's doing really great," Diana told my mom.

Again, Dungy said, "We have to get more details about a few things you mentioned."

I filled him in on details I had previously skimmed over, and remembered what the man said when I asked him to please leave my son alone. "He said, 'I'm a rapist, not a monster.'". Those words, along with the threats, ignited rage in my blackened soul.

When I exited the interview room for the final time, I got to see the four or five other people that were in the viewing room behind the mirror. Mixed in with those people was Investigator Kate Loken and Officer Renee Hewitt.

Diana was able to provide me with information and resources including how to submit receipts to the Minnesota Reparations Board to get refunded for the HIV medications. She was able to facilitate communication with people working on the case and offered to attend anything I needed her for.

She was also able to get me a phone to use while the investigators had mine as evidence. It was a prepaid phone (AKA, burner phone). Investigator Dungy had my phone to extract data to see if the rapist had tampered with anything. They initially said I'd have my phone back by the end of the week, but it was months and months before I saw it again.

I didn't miss my phone. I didn't miss Facebook, Instagram, or being tied to any social media platform. I didn't want anything to do with anyone outside of the small group of people I was in contact with. Given all that, the burner phone was perfect—a Motorola that came with one month of unlimited talk and text, and a small amount of data. I was overwhelmed with appreciation and gratitude, and so happy to have my own form of communication to chat with Erin, Cody, Jenny, my good friend Anne, and a few others.

THE DAYS CONTINUED TO PASS. I was making progress with my new norm, which consisted of hiding from the world and rebuilding my life. Little Man came back to stay with me again a week after the assault. My priority changed from myself to him and keeping him safe. As a single mother, I couldn't stay in zombie mode, I couldn't *not* be okay. I had to parent my son and I had to move forward.

During my final week off from work, James and I took a short trip with my aunt, uncle, and four-year-old cousin to Arizona. It was a trip we had planned six months prior, and it was James's first time on an airplane. He was thrilled. We had a great time together and it felt good to be away from Minnesota for a few days.

When we arrived back in Minnesota, I had received disappointing news from work about a promotion. I was going to be the Interim Nurse Manager while my boss was on maternity leave. Understandably, leadership didn't want to put more stress on me, so they decided it would be someone else. I wished I hadn't received this news in front of James because I cried an ugly but silent cry. I had been getting good at silent cries over the last couple of weeks. James was sitting right next to me and saw my tearful face and quivering lip. I was trying extremely hard to not let him see. He stood up from where he was sitting, stepped in front of me with his little-boy hands on my knees and said, "It's okay, Mommy. It's okay. These worker men are nice," referring to the workers outside of the plane. James thought I was crying because the "worker men" were bad guys like the man who had come to our house. I had inadvertently given James a completely inaccurate perspective of hard working men, just like his father. I hated myself for it but ultimately it was the only explanation I could come up with at the time.

"No, no, honey. It's not that. Mommy is just sad right now." *Because some unknown monster is ruining my life; this is because of what he did.* "It's going to be okay. I know these worker men are nice," I replied. I was heartbroken about work, heartbroken my son had to see me cry again, and heartbroken I'd made him think the worst about a hard-working class of men.

OVER THE ENSUING WEEKS, I would randomly Google my story and when news articles were posted, I noticed they included details I mentioned in my interview. *Was it public?* I'd tell my sister this and she kept saying, "Stay off the internet. Stop looking up articles."

But I couldn't.

It was my story. It was my life. It was the near-death of me and the inconceivable threats against my son. I hated that the media knew details, but it was a big reason why I kept searching the story. I wanted to know everything Minnesota knew. I wanted to be prepared for what people might assume or ask or suspect. Knowledge is power, and I wanted to be in control of anything I could.

. . .

ONE OF THE final things I had to consider during my time off was starting the process of selling my home—the house that used to be my home, rather. It was the house James grew up in, where he learned how to ride a bike without training wheels, and where we met our wonderful neighbors and best friends, Kaila and Brandon.

Cody had repainted the living room, kitchen, dining room, our bedroom, and I did the downstairs bathroom. We repainted the entire basement and I had redone the garage door entrance complete with a new doorknob and deadbolt. I had just finished updating the entire basement bathroom and was putting in the finishing touches the morning of Saturday, November 17. I had fixed the tub, installed a new shower head, patched holes in the wall, and hung new decorations and an entirely new light fixture.

Cody built the swing set in the backyard and spent so much time making our yard into a fluffy, green lawn instead of a moss pit. It was where our sweet dog, Marley lived and passed away. Every dent in the wall and scratch on the floor was ours. I didn't want to start over. But I had to.

8

It was hard for James to understand why we couldn't go back to our old house and play with the neighbors. There were times I thought James was struggling more than I was. Despite knowing about the "bad guy," he would ask why we couldn't go home, and every time he did, it somehow broke my heart into more pieces.

He struggled with figuring out who was a bad guy and who was a good guy. He seemed to not feel safe and he fed off my emotions, so I needed to stay strong. James and I were playing in the children's area at the mall one day when he saw a man wearing a neon yellow construction vest walk by. He ran to me, pointed at the man and said, "Mommy, look! A worker-man! Is that the worker-man who hurt you?"

Oh, honey. What have I done? What has this monster done?

He went through a period for about a week of acting out. He was hitting, throwing toys, not listening to me nor my family. He was usually a good listener and well behaved—as much as a three-year-old normally would—but as I was trying to figure out what was going on, I reminded myself this little boy had a safe, warm, cozy home he grew up in with his best friends next door, and one day we left and couldn't go back. He didn't have his toys, his own bed, his kitties, his bathroom, or his swing set. He was ripped from his home because it was now a crime scene. If the investigators didn't find the man who did this to us and we had stayed in that house, the rapist would always know where I live. He could always find me. We had no choice but to never go back.

James heard the man's voice. He heard the man talk to me through the door. He saw me cry hysterically as my mom called 911. Since he was acting out more than usual, something had to be going on that he didn't know how to articulate. He was a strong, spirited, independent, resilient boy, and I was going to make damn sure I did whatever it took to ensure he stayed that way. I decided to look into counseling for him just to be sure.

We also started a new routine for bedtime. We listened to each other's heart beat every night for months. I would listen to his, and he would listen to mine. *Thump-thump, thump-thump, thump-thump.* I cherished my little man and that beating heart of his. Even in those difficult moments, like when I was lying on the floor on my back with my eyes closed for a moment trying to relax and was brought back to reality by being body-slammed by my three-year-old... Even then, I cherished my little man who clearly didn't understand the laws of gravity yet.

9

INVESTIGATOR DUNGY INTERMITTENTLY FILLED ME IN ON ITEMS his team and the Bureau of Criminal Apprehension (BCA) had taken from my home, interesting clues they found, and the progress of the DNA being processed. I was more than willing to provide the investigators with any and all information they asked for.

When the BCA was at my house, they wanted to collect data from my internet. Because of this, I had to keep it on and paid for. My home would be a crime scene until they were completed with their work. Each time my family and friends went to my home to get me items (additional clothes for me, clothes for my son, medicine), they had a police escort go with them to check the home before they went in. I couldn't box up my things and get it ready to sell until the investigators and BCA were finished collecting evidence. I had to pay for my home mortgage, internet, and utilities even though I couldn't live there.

I had spent a lot of time browsing the internet searching sexual assault websites for advice, resources, and other stories similar to mine so I didn't have to feel alone. I often came across sites that showed statistics. They all agreed the average lifetime cost for a rape victim is over $122,000. One hundred grand in therapy, medicine, lost wages, new belongings, moving, and all the other expense that come with surviving an assault. The curveball in my case was I had no idea who the rapist was. So not only did I have the plethora of up-front costs, I also had to take measures to try to hide my son and I from the public for fear the rapist was watching our every move, waiting to attack again. It made me sad and confused to read only roughly one-third of survivors report their assault.

BEFORE MY SISTER had to go back to Kuwait, I brought her and her wife to a meeting that was arranged at the St. Charles Police Department for Investigator Dungy and me. They allowed me to park my car inside the police station so no one would see me enter the building. Dungy met me in a conference room and turned on his tape recorder.

"How have things been since we last talked? Has anything changed? Has anyone new come to mind that you think could've done this?" he asked.

"No, we haven't thought of anyone else. I got a new car," I offered, knowing it was irrelevant but wanting to lighten the conversation for a moment. I had no new information to offer so my sister was brought into the room and I was escorted out. When their short interview was done, Investigator Dungy brought us all into the room.

"I have a couple of photos here I want to show you guys. One of our police officers saw a vehicle in a field drive by your house on the night of November 16," he said to me.

"The Friday night before?" I questioned.

"Yeah. The same vehicle was also seen parked at the Catholic Church the next night, on the seventeenth. The pastor of the church saw two vehicles in the parking lot." Dungy pulled two photos out of a folder and set them in front of me.

"There was a blue iced-over truck parked there that resembles this style of vehicle. Does this look familiar to you? This one was seen parked at the church on the seventeenth." I didn't know anyone with a vehicle that color and style, neither did my sister. The Catholic Church was about a quarter of a mile east from my house, separated from my neighborhood by a field.

"How about this one?" It was a maroon Buick SUV.

I paged through my mind like it was an encyclopedia, trying to pinpoint anyone who drove a vehicle like that. Well, my mom, for starters. Other than her, I couldn't think of anyone. It was such a common vehicle; I could easily be overthinking it. My sister couldn't think of anyone either.

"This is the color and style of vehicle that was seen parked in a field drive up the road from your house on the sixteenth and then in the church parking lot on the seventeenth," he explained.

"Two nights in a row?" I questioned.

"Yes. We have reason to believe he was in your house Friday night as well."

...what?

How? Why? What?! I was mortified and confused and furious. So many emotions flooded my body. Dungy pulled out his laptop and showed us something mesmerizing: drone footage of the rapist's path he took to my house from where he parked at the church.

As the aerial footage appeared on the screen, Dungy elaborated. "There were two trails in the field. One was from the field drive to your house; the other was from the church parking lot to your house. The trail from the field drive was snowed over a little bit, as though the path was taken Friday night. The second trail was fresh."

I felt myself grow pale. My heart sank to the floor and I felt vomit creeping up my throat. *Am I going to pass out?* Amy put her hand on my shoulder. *He came to my house the night before the assault.*

Reality struck. *I. Was. Hunted.*

I didn't know this at the time, but Deputy Charles Rolbiecki helped with the case as well. He went to my house after my mom had called 911 to assist the St. Charles Police Department. He was crucial in locating boot prints around my house and tracked them to the area of the church and the field drive where the tire tracks were located. There was also a glove print found near my basement window.

Erin, Amy, and I tried to process the information. We asked a couple of questions, discussed the vehicle that was seen, and had more information to think about now. When we left, we called Cody right away to fill him in. I wanted him to know everything I knew. And naturally, we were seeing maroon SUVs everywhere. Everyone was a suspect.

THE LITTLE THINGS that happened during this time ended up being big things I'd always remember. I was in the midst of getting a dental implant at Main Street Dental Clinic in the winter of 2018. I had an appointment with Dr. Osman Swedeh. He was going to remove my bridge and check how the implant was healing before we proceeded with the final stages.

When I arrived at the appointment, I became emotional. I was supposed to be taking good care of the first part of my implant (the screw in my bone) and flossing under the bridge religiously. Since the attack, I hadn't been doing that. Normal things I should have been doing as a daily routine left my world and I had to reconstruct my life. I had to try to remember how to live day after day when I was so consumed with pain. In doing so, I obviously didn't remember everything. I didn't bring any of my dental supplies for my bridge to my aunt's house.

"Danielle Leukam?" an assistant called.

I stood and walked back to the room, but with each step I took, I became more nervous about what was happening under my bridge that I hadn't been taking proper care of. I was supposed to get the final pieces in the beginning of 2019.

And then I broke down in the dentist's office.

"I'm so sorry. I don't know what it looks like under there. I don't have my things. I don't have a house. I don't have my floss, and I don't have anything. I'm so sorry," the words poured out and I was extremely embarrassed. It came out of nowhere. I was sure the assistant was thinking, *What is wrong with this woman?*

"A man broke into my house. I had to move. I'm so sorry," I somehow managed to mutter. I wasn't supposed to be talking about what I endured, but it was too late. Thank goodness for HIPPA, right?

"Oh, honey. Oh, no. Let me go talk to Dr. Swedeh." The dental assistant was kind and genuine. She asked me if I was okay before going into the other room.

Dr. Swedeh came in a few moments later and said, "We don't have to look under the bridge today. We can do that next time. Let's reschedule. Are you okay?"

"Yes, I'm so sorry. I didn't mean to cry. I'm sorry. I feel so stupid," I replied, ashamed of myself.

Dr. Swedeh made sure I was well taken care of by the dental assistant. She grabbed a couple of little bags and stuffed them full of supplies to send with me. I would have everything I needed to take care of my implant.

As I left the office with my bags full of supplies, I was overcome with gratitude for these people—essentially strangers—who showed me such kindness. It became a small step toward regaining trust in people.

. . .

ON DECEMBER TENTH OF 2018, I returned to work. I was happy to be going back, but apprehensive about the journey and how vulnerable I would be.

The morning of my first day back, I had gotten a ride in with Jenny and stayed by her side on the walk across the skyway from the parking ramp into work. When we got to our department, it was hard to make eye contact with people. I didn't want anyone to ask me why I was off for three weeks. I wanted to be left alone, but at the same time, I didn't want to be alone. I always looked over my shoulder and paid close attention to who was walking behind me. When someone came into the office I was working in, I would stand up and turn around. I had to make sure no one was directly behind me. I would suction myself to the side in elevators, stay close to the wall when walking down the hallway, and avoid the employee cafeteria that could have a couple hundred people in it at any given time. *What if he works here? What if he knows I told? What if he's been waiting for me to return to work?*

Despite my concerns and the fact that I was going to be out in the open and exposed to the world, it was good for me to return to work. I was glad to see my work family, and I finally felt like I had purpose again. Everyone was happy to see me back to work and appearing to be well. And that first day, Jenny didn't let me leave her side the whole day. If she had to step away, she would send someone else to watch over me.

There were a handful of people who knew what had happened, including a few doctors, (the Department Chair, Dr. Leibovich, and the Practice Chair, Dr. Gettman, for security purposes) nurses, and a couple of close desk operation specialists, my dear friends. I was grateful to have my friends watching out for me. It was hard to admit I liked having a babysitter that first day, but I sincerely *didn't* want to be alone. I was also glad hardly anyone gave me a hard time for being gone from work for three weeks. Only a couple of people said, "Hope you had a nice long vacation!" and, "Why were you off for so long?" It was hard to respond to things like that on the fly, but I improvised my way through it.

I emailed my job's security department upon returning to work. That same day, the interim security supervisor came to the floor to meet with me.

"Hi, I'm Elizabeth," she said.

"Thank you for coming. I'm Danielle," I replied. Her presence encompassed me with comfort and warmth. She was dressed like a leader and presented with the utmost professionalism, but I specifically remember her soft, concerned eyes.

"I'm so sorry for what happened to you. Should we sit down and talk? Then we can figure out how best to make you feel safe."

I did not hesitate to share my story with her. At this point, I had gone through the story so many times with investigators and close family that I felt cold and detached as I was speaking.

"What resources have you looked into so far?" she asked.

"I have a victim's advocate who has been helping me with some of that. I'm saving receipts to turn into the reparations board." Elizabeth had an excellent resume. She had a lot of experience in the field and proved to be thorough and competent. I quickly grew to learn how strong and amazing she was.

"Do you feel safe at work today?" she asked.

"Well, I don't know. I mean, I don't think it was anyone from this department that hurt me," I replied, not knowing how to verbalize the terror I felt without sounding overly dramatic.

"Okay, how about anyone else? Any patients? Other departments?" she asked.

"No, nothing I can think of. I guess my biggest concern is walking to work and going back to my car alone. What if he's watching me? What if he knows where I work? I walk five blocks outside from the parking lot I park in," I explained. Coming to work with my boss was unfortunately not going to be a long-term solution. She normally put in sixty hours a week, when I put in forty to forty-five hours. She'd be going on maternity leave in a few months too.

"I can't make any promises, but I will check into getting you a parking spot in the employee ramp. For now, when you park in your parking lot, you can have security pick you up. They would be more than happy to escort you to work and back to your car afterwards," she said. I didn't want to cause any inconveniences. But at the same time, I didn't want to be a lone sheep in the middle of a field. I didn't want to walk alone or walk outside on those dark, winter mornings or after work when the sun was setting.

Being in public, having people walk behind me, being in an elevator with men, and walking down long hallways with no cameras all made me feel unsafe, but I didn't think it was worth bringing up to her. Nothing felt entirely safe. In the months to come, Elizabeth would continue to be one of my biggest and most consistent advocates.

BEING at work left me feeling vulnerable and exposed. I was no longer in hiding. I was straight-up scared—heart racing, sweating, and near panic attacks every day. I paid attention to men's hands, their noses, their stature, and their shoulders. I looked at them and picked apart everything I thought I might recognize and either labeled them as a potential suspect or ruled them out. Thankfully, I was able to rule out most of my male coworkers. Obvious characteristics were age, stature, skin color and accents. Those I couldn't rule out, I would keep my eye on.

Focusing on work went better than I expected. It was a good distraction, and I could escape (for the most part) from having to continually try to process what happened. At work, I was no longer entirely numb. The red, green, and silver Christmas garland in the nurses' workroom, the classic Christmas music playing, and my co-workers' smiles and "Good morning" greetings helped me feel back at home.

Tight clothing continued to make me feel uncomfortable. Every day I'd wear a scrub jacket over my scrub top as part of my way of hiding. I didn't want my figure to be visible through my clothes. I didn't want to have a feminine body. I would have worn a snow suit to hide if I could have. I didn't want anyone to feel attracted to me and I wanted that target on my forehead gone for good.

When my shoe would come untied at work, I had to be either in a corner or in an empty room to bend down to re-tie it. I would fidget with the button on the front of my scrub coat and cross my arms when walking down a hallway. I wanted to keep my head down at all times. I kept wishing to myself, *Please don't notice me.*

I DIDN'T HAVE Brian's phone number memorized since we hadn't been dating long, nor did I have Facebook anymore, so I sent him an email letting him know what happened. We corresponded back and forth but never made time to meet up again. I knew Brian wasn't the man from that morning, but I wasn't ready to be away from home or work yet. I kept busy trying to settle into this temporary stage of my life and ultimately our relationship fizzled.

I missed his kindness and companionship. We had fun listening to music, drinking wine, and simply just hanging out, but I couldn't continue to keep a hold on him knowing I wasn't in a place to give him what he deserved.

A COUPLE of weeks later I received a request to meet with Investigator Dungy and Anne who worked for the City Police Department in Winona. I was happy to get this call because I was looking forward to an update on the case. Anne was just as nice as Mark and made me feel safe. I had a lot of confidence in her.

Investigator Dungy and Anne met me in the parking lot of the Government Center in Olmsted County, close to where I was working.

"How are you, Danielle?" Anne asked.

I'm dying inside. I wish I could keep my little boy with me twenty-four seven to protect him. I want to put myself into a cocoon until this is all over with. I want more time to heal. But instead I replied, "I'm okay." I replied.

After introductions and small talk, Dungy got down to business. "We gathered a list of people based on your most recent contacts in your phone. Just let us know how you know each one of them and when you saw them last."

Wow, a real list of suspects. Did this mean we were closer to pinpointing who it was? I was excited to be moving forward. One step closer to him being behind bars, I hoped. There were people on the list my aunt, my sister and I had come up with already.

One name popped up I didn't recognize at first. But then it came to me, "Oh, yeah," fear filled my body. "I met Jeff on a dating app. We chatted for a while, but I never met up with him. I never told him where I lived. He was a hunting guide." *Click—a hunting guide... a hunter. A stalker?* ˋ

"Do you have your password for the dating app?" Dungy asked.

"Of course, absolutely." I provided them with my passwords. I wanted them to have access to anything and everything they needed. *Here is the key to my entire life. Look at anything. Please save me.* All concerns for having privacy in these regards were non-existent. They would check into this guy for sure but continued to move down the list.

We moved on to the next name and I said, "Yeah, he's a creep. But he doesn't know where I live."

"Could he have followed you from somewhere? Does he know where you work?" Anne questioned.

"Yeah, I guess so." Anything was a possibility. Everyone was a suspect. I felt like most of the people on the list had made a pass at me that I had denied so maybe it was someone who was bitter.

As we were chatting, I got a message from Brian saying investigators had just left his house. There were teams of people out doing interviews in the area. I couldn't believe the hard work they were doing and the dedication they had. It was overwhelming and comforting, but nothing could stop me from looking over my shoulder.

I WAS ASKED to go to the Winona County Law Enforcement Center to give my fingerprints.

"Will you come with me?" I asked Cody. I didn't want to go alone; I had never been there before.

"Of course," he agreed.

When we arrived, the officer at the desk was expecting me.

"Do you want me to go with you?" Cody asked when the officer was leading me into the back room.

"I'll be okay... thank you." But *thank you* wasn't enough. *With my whole heart, thank you,* is what I meant. I told him I would be fine. I knew he would be on the other side of the door waiting for me and I felt safe there.

The officer took two sets of my fingerprints on a red inkless pad. As it turns out, they found a fingerprint on my silver water cup and wanted to rule out that it was mine. It was the cup he grabbed when he intended to give me something—drugs, I still assumed.

. . .

A FEW DAYS later Dungy briefly updated me on their progress. They never told me *everything*, but the most important piece of information was, "The DNA results came back."

"Really?" I was shocked and excited there was progress made.

"There was male DNA found from the rape kit. There was also male DNA found on some things from your house," he explained. "It was found on the guns that were in your laundry basket. But this doesn't mean a whole lot right now. We still have to link the DNA with someone. We'll run it through the database to see if there is a match. We'll be collecting samples from suspects who don't have a solid alibi."

I had to keep all of this information to myself, with the exception of my close family and Cody. Unlike the crime shows you see on TV, DNA results do not come back that same day, or even that week. We were lucky to get these results back about a month later. It took what seemed like forever. They had to collect it, send it in, get it into the appropriate hands and the DNA experts had to process it.

Every step forward renewed my hope for finding this monster.

10

CHRISTMAS WAS BY FAR MY FAVORITE TIME OF THE YEAR. I LOVED the lights, music, spirit, and decorations. This year I couldn't see how I could possibly celebrate Christmas when my world was so dark. Two of my girlfriends, Anne and Tessa, wanted to bring my Christmas spirit back. We met up at Roosters in Rochester where I wore a boot knife, a pocketknife, and had a third knife in my purse within easy reach right next to my pepper spray. We had a drink and ordered dinner.

"We have a little gift for you," Anne said. She and Tessa went to their cars and returned with two baskets of gifts. I was floored.

"What? You guys! You didn't need to do this. Really." I didn't want to be a charity case but seeing my two girlfriends in their ugly Christmas sweaters holding these baskets showed me what an amazing support system I had. There was wine, books (including a book from one of my favorite authors, Allen Eskens), and toys for James and me to play with together.

"This is incredible. I don't know what to say." I was speechless. The next thing I saw was a snow globe. I *loved* snow globes and all of mine were sitting in my crime-scene house in St. Charles. It was red on the bottom and inside was a flag and a saluting soldier who resembled my sister. Erin had already returned to Kuwait and I missed her dearly. I turned the dial and shook the globe. The snow and glitter floated around the soldier and flag while it played Amazing Grace, and this was when I broke down. Warm, salty tears streamed down my face, and I cried because of my gratitude for life and friends and this amazing support I wasn't sure I deserved.

Amazing Grace, how sweet the sound.
That saved a wretch like me.
I once was lost, but now am found.
Was blind, but now I see.

We spent the remainder of the evening playing pool and this is where I met my sister's good friend, her military brother, Jake. He had such a kind and confident demeanor when he first introduced himself after recognizing I was Erin's sister. Anyone who my sister trusted, I could trust, so I knew he was a good man.

Jake and I grew to be best friends over time. He was the support person I spent the most time with through the aftermath and he helped me rebuild my life, stronger than it was before. He had become my number one fan and I wouldn't be where I am today without him.

James and I went to the store the next day and bought a big pack of triple-A batteries so we could play remote-control bumper cars and a fishing game. We spent nearly an hour playing with the bumper cars in my aunt's kitchen, laughing every time we would hit each other and our little guys would fly out of the cars. It was heart-warming to see him smile and laugh again.

My friend Katie had sent a box of books, goodies, and toys for us to play together as well. She sent so much that each day James would get to open a new toy. During a time I felt hopeless and lonely, the joy in his face brought back light into my soul.

But the fun and games weren't endless. When James and I would get ready to go out of the house, he watched my pocket knife go in my pocket and my blade go in my boot. "Mommy, you can use your knife on bad guys," he innocently stated.

How do I respond to that?

"Or... in case we need to cut something with a sharp knife," I replied then quickly tried to redirect the conversation to something else. I wanted to protect my son physically, but also from the truth as to what happened that morning. I feared he would never feel safe again if he knew everything that happened. This was a realization for me that I needed to get him in to see a counselor.

Back at work, Dr. Leibovich knew of another doctor who had a place I could stay so I didn't have to live between my aunt's and parents' houses. Dr. Thompson sent me an email and offered me use of their family's townhome in a small town outside of Rochester until I found a more permanent location. It took me a while to consider, because again, I didn't want to accept charity. However, they reiterated the townhome was sitting empty until its owners came back to town at the end of March.

I accepted their offer and on January 2, I got to move into what would be my temporary home. It was a secret safe house where no one except close family and friends would know where I was living.

It was a beautiful four-bedroom, three and a half-bathroom townhome in one of the safest neighborhoods in the area. The home had a huge, dreamy master bedroom and bathroom. It was more than James and I could have ever dreamed of. Dr. Thompson also did research on security systems. He landed on SimpliSafe and bought a system he was going to have installed in the house on the day I moved in.

Here I was packing up my stuff in a garbage bag and laundry basket to go in between homes, and now I would have a beautiful place of my own with my son. This gave me enough time to sell my crime scene house and buy a new one. I was apprehensive about living on my own, but the security system helped me feel safe. My address would be confidential through Minnesota's Safe at Home program the Olmsted County victim's advocate told me about.

On my first night at the safe house, my boss Jenny helped me settle in. Dr. Leibovich brought over groceries, and Dr. Thompson gave Jenny and I a tour of the neighborhood and mentioned a couple of police officers who lived in the area as well.

One of the first things I did when I got settled in was take a long bubble bath with a glass of wine, candles, and Netflix, forcing myself to try to relax.

AFTER MY HOME was done being a crime-scene, my family, friends and I got it ready to sell. It took me a long time to even consider going back to the house, but I didn't want my family to have to do it all for me. That wasn't my style and I wanted to be useful; I couldn't be completely dependent. I soon realized how hard it was to be there. I cried, reminisced, but most of all, I was absolutely angry.

Pushing aside my rage, we cleaned the mess the man left, boxed up the clutter, and moved it to a storage unit in Rochester. We left the furniture and wall decorations, including the master bedroom bed and furniture. I was working with wonderful realtors who staged my home to get it ready to sell. They hired a photographer, and my home was officially on the market.

I received a text from the realtors at work the afternoon of Wednesday, January 16, 2019. When I first saw the text that my home was officially on the market, I was excited; time to move forward. But then I clicked on the link that showed my house staged, on the market, and ready to be bought by some other family. I started scrolling through the photos while I was at work thinking it would be no big deal but then a trickle of tears quickly turned into sobs.

My co-worker Don was passing by my office and stopped to ask, "Are you okay? Can I get someone for you?"

"No, I'm fine," I managed to get out in between sobs. I was obviously not okay, but I didn't want to admit it.

"Are you sure? Want me to go get Jenny or someone?" he asked.

I knew Jenny was in a meeting and wasn't available.

"Will you get Leah?" I finally gave in.

Leah was one of my friends from work who knew my situation. She was strong, experienced, and tough; I was glad to have her in my corner. She came to my office right away.

I didn't turn around when she walked in but managed to verbalize, "My house is on the market and I don't want to sell it. It's my home. It wasn't my choice; I don't want to sell it."

She rubbed my back and knew the exact words to say that helped me regain my composure, "I know, honey. But it's time for a fresh start. You're going to make any house you live in a *home* for you and James."

I can't say I was ready for a fresh start with a new home, but I didn't have a choice. I had to embrace the changes I was enduring.

11

ON A BITTERLY COLD DAY OVER TWO MONTHS AFTER THE ASSAULT, I met with Investigators Dungy and Loken. They had run the DNA through state and federal databases and unfortunately it didn't match with anyone who had DNA on file. Even Jeff the hunting guide wasn't a match. He already had DNA on file because of previous crimes he had committed. I hated hearing this information and it felt like a huge setback, but I knew they were still hard at work. They had ruled out a few people and started looking deeper into others.

Investigator Dungy had a piece of paper in his hand and he laid it on the table seemingly hesitant about what he wanted to say. He turned over the papers and slid them across the table in front of me and said, "We have results from the urine sample you gave in the ER. Your urine results show Methamphetamines."

...I'm sorry, what?

"What? I don't understand," I said as horror filled my body.

"Your urine test came back positive for meth, but your blood test came back negative. This means it metabolized out of your system, but it stays longer in your urine. So I'd like to go over the days prior to the incident with you," he explained.

I was in denial. He must have the wrong girl. *I'm Danielle. You're thinking of someone else, clearly,* I thought.

It *had* to be a false positive or, "If *he* was on meth, could that have shown in my urine sample from his bodily fluids?" I tried to make sense of this. My rage was growing, and I was realizing he *didn't* have the wrong girl. They were *my* results.

"We called the lab to see if there was any way your test could have come back positive from his body fluids. We also checked to see if it could have been a false positive," Dungy explained. "It wasn't a false positive, and your test couldn't have come back positive from his body fluids being on you." He went on to explain that they had taken a fine-tooth comb through my house, my phone, and my life and nothing raised a red flag indicating I was a meth user.

"Good. I don't have anything to hide. Look through whatever you want," I felt like I needed to convince them, a defense attorney, and eventually maybe a jury that I was in fact *not* a meth user. "I don't even know what meth looks like. That's not my style. That's not my character. You can ask *anyone* to verify that. Call my sister, Cody, my boss—anyone." I became increasingly angry considering how and why meth could have been in my system.

As soon as our meeting was over, I hopped on Google. Supposedly meth *can* be used as a form of a date rape drug, tricking girls into giving consent to have sexual intercourse because of the high they experience, per some of my findings. I don't remember ever feeling like I had been on drugs; I don't remember feeling high or jittery like I couldn't sleep.

Then I got to thinking... *What if I was on drugs as I was driving with my son in the car? What if I was under its effects while caring for him or while I was at work?* My mind wandered to how he had given me the drugs... and questioned, *What if James had accidentally been drugged instead of me? They had proof he was in my house the night before. He must have put the meth in something I ingested. Maybe that was what he wanted to give me when he was there?*

I was beyond furious. I was fuming, raging, seeing red, confused, and I felt completely violated all over again.

What if I had overdosed and died? What if my son had overdosed and died? What if I experienced withdrawal symptoms? What if I did something out of control that could have put my son at risk?

I had never been in trouble a day in my life with exception of *one* minor speeding ticket, and now they found meth in my system. I felt like I—you know, the *victim*—needed to defend myself. But knowing this information, I was able to narrow down the list of suspects for the investigators. I easily, without hesitation, listed three people whom I knew had done meth in the past.

I was not emotionally stable enough to go back to work right away so I called Cody. He was working in the area as a pipefitter, installing fire protection in new areas of the hospital. He met up with me for a few minutes and had such a calm demeanor that it wore off on me enough that I was able to go back to work and function as the charge nurse I was being paid to be. I had to go back to putting out fires, making schedules for forty-five nurses, and putting my personal issues aside.

THE NEXT MORNING I was on the phone with dispatch requesting a police escort to daycare. I was taking every safety precaution offered to me, and this was not the first time I had gotten an escort. The dispatch lady had multiple questions for me, which seemed never ending. The way she worded her questions made me feel stupid, like I shouldn't have been calling. After continual, condescending questions I finally said, "Every time I call, it takes fifteen minutes for me to explain my situation as to why I'd like an escort *while* I have my son in the car. Every. Single. Day." By the time I would have gotten off the phone, I would have already been at the daycare center. They told me not to call too soon, and obviously I couldn't call too late, so the time I had to call was during the forty-minute drive from the safe house to his daycare.

This must have made her upset because she said things that made me feel even worse. At the end of the conversation, she had made me feel like a complete idiot and was taking out her anger or her fatigue on me. I then replied with one-word phrases, and we hung up.

The first thing I did was take my anger out on the steering wheel. I called Cody and started tearing up as the phone rang through my car speakers. It was the Journey song, "Don't Stop Believin'." He had told me to call him if I needed to talk, so he was the first person I thought of when I was completely outraged.

My tears and frustration included the rage I had bottled up since the day prior when I found out there was meth in my system. "I'm just so mad! I don't understand. Why is this so stupid? Why do I have to tell them every single time I call?" I was on fire.

Cody listened and told me exactly what I needed to hear. "Well, tell the officer that meets you at the daycare she was terrible, file a complaint. You don't deserve to be talked to like that." He was validating my emotions, regardless of how irrational they were.

"Okay. Yeah. But I don't even want to call them anymore. I don't want to do this every fricking day."

"I know. Tell them how you feel. Tell the person who meets you at the daycare." I hung up with Cody and an officer called me.

I answered, "Hello?"

"Hi, ma'am. I'm Officer Smith. I understand you're looking to have an escort to drop off your son." he said.

"Yeah. And I get you guys need to know why, but I don't understand why I have to tell you the entire story every time I call. I'd rather pull my son out of daycare and stop calling all together than risk talking to that dispatch lady again. Seriously. I'm done. I don't deserve that, and I don't want my son to hear this." *I'm sure I was overreacting.* The officer was genuinely nice and understanding. More importantly, he didn't make me feel like an idiot or condescend me. He offered me a dispatch case number so when I called again, I could provide this number and they would have some background information regarding the case. I thanked him for his time, and we hung up.

THE OFFICER then met me at daycare and waited in his vehicle. After I was done bringing my son inside, I went back to my car, and he called my cell phone to ask if I had a few minutes to chat.

It was negative seventeen degrees Fahrenheit, but I didn't mind one bit because I had words to say, and he needed to hear them. I got out of my car to greet him and started with, "I probably overreacted with the dispatch call lady, but I'm sick of having to explain myself every single time I call in front of my son."

The officer understood, and again was kind.

"You have a case number now so when you call, give them that number so they can look up your case without you having to relive your story."

When we parted our ways, he turned and said, "Good luck," in a genuine manner. I appreciated hearing that because I sure as hell would need it. *I'd really like my son and I to stay alive.*

Fear of the unknown must have been causing uncontrollable spurts of anger. New information, potential new leads, and a new sense of being violated caused a deeper, greater rage. I was completely on edge and hoped nothing would push me over it.

I knew in these moments it was best I had seen a psychologist earlier that week (finally) and it was good that I was going to see her again the following week. When I first met Licensed Psychologist, Gina Dilly, I did not want to be there. I didn't want to admit defeat or admit I needed help. I also did not want to have to go through telling my entire story again, but our initial meeting was great. She introduced herself, showed interest in me and my story, showed compassion, and validated my thoughts. She asked what I wanted to work on, and I explained PTSD and anger. I was able to put on a happy face at work, but I was boiling inside. Gina and I had set another meeting date for the following week, and I was surprisingly looking forward to it. She was a neutral person who validated my feelings and helped me learn how to process and work through my anger.

THURSDAY WAS the day I found out I had been drugged, Friday was the dispatch call from hell, and Saturday was the day my patience was tested with an acquaintance.

Kelsey lived in a nearby town and had somehow known about the assault through small-town gossip. After normal chit chat, she brought up the attack and said to me, "What were you thinking? What was going through your head? I mean, how could you let him do that to you? I would have beat his ass."

Excuse me, what?

"There's no way I would have let that happen," she continued. "It would have been a murder scene, not a crime scene."

What have I done? Should I have fought? Did I let him do this to me? Did I let him do this to my son? Did I allow this to happen? Is she right?

My heart dropped from my chest to the floor. My face

turned white and I felt like I was in the wrong. No one had said anything like this to me before. I was held hostage at gunpoint in my home, tied up, raped, and had my child's life threatened for my cooperation, but was it my fault? Then I remembered the gun in my face the moment the light from my phone met the end of my bed. How quickly my hands were zip tied behind my back. He knew how to get into my home and threatened to go to my son's school to murder him if I told. Then I remembered we survived.

Doing what she said she would have done would have certainly woken up a sleeping child and it would have brought him into the mix as an easy target. But my son's innocent little heart is still beating to this day and so is mine, so obviously I did something right. But on top of what I later learned to be victim blaming, she also made me feel awful regarding my ex-husband, blaming me as the reason he would drink instead of taking medications for anxiety.

After my interaction with her, I felt sick to my stomach. I cried most of the drive home and pulled over to the side of the road because I couldn't see. I almost threw up. I was glad James didn't have to see me like this. I had to call Cody. I hurt him when I said we should separate, which she also reminded me of, and I hated how everything was my fault.

"Hello?"

"I'm so sorry. I'm so sorry this happened. I'm sorry I hurt you. I'm sorry I wanted to separate. I don't want to be apart. I don't. I'm sorry I wasn't good. She...! She...!"

"Danielle, what's going on?" he asked, concerned.

"Kelsey said, 'How could you let this happen? How could you let him do that to you?'" The pain consuming my mind, heart and soul made me physically hurt and I became hysterical. It made me feel responsible for what happened, and I *allowed* this to happen to me with my son in the house. I questioned, *How am I worthy enough to be alive? I hurt the love of my life. I allowed bad things to happen to me. I allowed someone to threaten to murder my child. I am nothing but pain. Why should I even be living anymore?*

I took her words to heart, where they stabbed me like a knife over and over. I was being blamed for being tied up at gunpoint and raped. *How could you let this happen? How could you let him do that to you?*

"Danielle, we're past that," he didn't offer much else other than simply what happened was not my fault. But I felt like I didn't deserve his time anyway. I didn't deserve to have him console me even after I was brutally victim blamed. And truthfully, I wasn't emotionally stable enough to go through with a divorce when I did, and I wished so many times that I hadn't. He was friends with Kelsey and seemed as though he didn't want to say she was wrong.

It frightened me that an acquaintance knew what happened. If there was gossip going around, what if the rapist heard about it too? He would be furious, and he'd certainly be looking to kill me. On top of her making me feel awful, word was getting out.

Maybe he already knows. Maybe he already went back to my house, only to find I wasn't there. These thoughts of horror filled my mind. But not only that day, it was every day. It was every moment that my mind wasn't consumed with something else like work or playing with my son.

I MET with Gina again the following Tuesday. The building was cold and old, but it still held character. Her office was housed on the second floor of an old brick building in downtown Rochester, like a diamond in the rough. Walking into her office made me feel warm and welcome. The music was soothing, the lights were low, and Gina's presence was calming.

"Last week we talked about what happened to you back in

November. You still don't know who the rapist is, and you're experiencing a lot of rage and anger. We were able to work through some of your anger. How have you been since we last saw each other?" Gina asked.

I had no idea where to start. I thought I should just be honest. "Well, the defense is going to make me seem like a drug user," I told her, referring to the meth that was found in my system. I filled her in on my three days of hell.

"Danielle, what you are feeling is normal. Let's talk about the stages of grief," she said, laying them out for me. I realized I was able to relate, particularly to the anger stage.

"Last time we met, you were calm, cool, and collected. You seemed disconnected from the incident, but that is a good thing. This is a safety mechanism your brain is doing to help you cope with what happened." I felt like she was listening to me, and thought I had a good head on my shoulders. I couldn't believe she was able to put the situation into such accurate words. When I needed to seem normal, I was fantastic at acting that way. I had to disconnect from the incident to suppress my rage. But tucking it away wasn't making it *go* away.

"You did the right thing. You saved yourself. You saved your son. Those things that girl said to you were victim blaming, one hundred percent. What happened was *not* your fault. The only person to blame is the person that broke into your home," she reassured me. When I left our meeting, I felt confident. I felt ready to take on another day of hell if I had to.

12

The housing market around Rochester, Minnesota was competitive. It was especially competitive annually between March and July. There were multiple new apartment complexes where rent was $1200 to $1600 a month—more than my mortgage was in St. Charles. March was when the competition and bidding wars could often be against ten other people and you had to bid $10,000 more than the asking price listed to even have your offer considered.

I couldn't do the competition, so I broadened my search to surrounding areas. I found a house on the first of February that I knew could be my home. It was small but just what James and I needed to get by. I decided to put in an offer after looking at it with my mom and realtors. Turns out, there were multiple offers, so the sellers were going to wait until the following Monday morning to make a decision.

On Sunday night, I was thinking about what I was going to hear the next morning once the sellers reviewed the offers. I found myself seeing red again. I was mad I was even in this situation. If they didn't accept my offer, I'd have to move back in with my parents and aunt until another place came up that was in my price range. In just two months, the owners of the town-home I was staying in would be coming back to town.

I was like shattered glass barely holding myself together, waiting for one small touch to make me fall to pieces. I broke apart often now, but I would lift my chin after regaining my composure, put myself back together, and march on. I put one foot in front of the other with strength and determination I never knew I had. I credit learning this from my mom and practicing it myself because of my little boy.

MONDAY MORNING CAME AROUND and just like any other day, I put on a smile at work and pretended like I was a normal human being. It was the same thing I did for my son. At ten-thirty a.m. I peeked at my phone as it vibrated on my desk. My realtor's name popped up; I received a text message with a snapshot that said, *Congratulations...* I immediately opened the message to learn I had bought a new home! The sellers accepted my offer, and the house would be mine.

I instantly felt a huge weight lift off my shoulders. No more looking at homes online, no more looking at homes in negative thirty-degree weather, and no more stress about what was going to happen come the end of March when I had to move out of the safe house. James and I would have a house we would make our home. I wish I could have bought the beautiful temporary safe house I was living in. I felt like a queen in that bedroom and huge bathroom, but unfortunately it was not for sale.

My tainted home in St. Charles sold as well. I realized there was no way I could take my bed and frame with though. I'd have to buy a new bed frame, mattress, nightstands, and dresser. I became angry again when I thought about having to buy new bedroom furniture. I don't like to spend a lot of money, particularly on items that were just fine... But there was no way in hell I would bring those polluted items into my new home. They would be triggers every night before bed and every morning when I woke up. So the decision was made, the bedroom furniture would stay in the house, and the mattress would go into a storage shed until the weather was good enough for me to watch it burn.

13

Here is an abbreviated list of how that morning has affected my life. The list is fluid. Things resolve, but more troubles arise, and issues I would have never thought of pop in out of nowhere.

1. I had PTSD.
2. My finances were plummeting.
3. I had to move.
4. I had to buy a new vehicle.
5. We had to hide from the world.
6. My son was grieving and had an obsession with bad guys.
7. I had difficulty trusting people short term.
8. I had difficulty rusting people long term.
9. I had to take medications and manage their side effects.
10. My relationship with my family suffered.
11. I lost a promotion.
12. I drank more. Let's be real; it was every day. I never had prior.

13. I didn't exercise *near* as much as I used to.
14. I lacked feeling safe.
15. I lack feeling like my son was safe.
16. I needed a confidential address and had to deal with the inconveniences of that.
17. I needed therapy.
18. I struggled with anger, rage, and hostility.
19. I felt unworthy.
20. I suffered with brokenness, heartache, and pain that would take years to heal, if at all.

I HAVE PTSD. I didn't realize this until one day it hit me like a ton of bricks.

My boss had organized a professional development day at work. All nurses were scheduled to go, half in the morning, the other half in the afternoon. I was assigned to go in the morning. One of the education sessions during the day was a campaign called "Stop the Bleed." I had no idea what this was about, but I was about to find out.

The speaker started the presentation with a YouTube video of a man at his place of work. He appeared to be angry. There was a picture of a gun, and my heart instantly started pounding. I was surrounded by my co-workers and most of them had no idea of my story, but I suddenly felt like all eyes were on me, along with a burning, hot spotlight. I felt vulnerable and unsafe. The video showed the man shooting his coworkers.

The blood splattering on the wall is what pushed me over the edge; I bolted out of the room. I was embarrassed, deep in fight or flight mode that caused me extreme disarray at work in front of my coworkers including my nursing administrator and operations manager.

A moment later Jenny came out as I was shaking with bone

chattering chills, hyperventilating as I broke into sobs. I felt stupid and mortified. It was like a tsunami of unease came over me and tried to drown me. I should have been able to control myself. Jenny embraced me in an "I'm so sorry, it will be okay," hug. I felt her heart pounding too, trying to heal my PTSD. We connected in that moment, and it helped me calm the panic.

I didn't go back into the presentation, but rather took a long walk with the operations manager until it came time to test-out on how to use a tourniquet. What did my coworkers think? Did they know why I ran out of the room and didn't come back? Did they think I was childish for not being able to watch a video of someone shooting someone else? Shame consumed me; I wished it had never happened.

Once I was calm, I returned to the room and tested on the skills. And again, I marched on with the rest of my day. I had a job to do. I had a life to live. He took control of my life that morning and I needed to figure out how to get it back.

RATHER THAN GOING to a public gym where I would be accessible to him, I took up drinking. I had been drinking one to three drinks every night since the assault. Maybe only one time I had gone a day without alcohol because I tried coping "on my own." Now don't get me wrong, I wouldn't get drunk. That wasn't my style, and I *always* needed to be able to take care of James.

I wanted to change. I thought I wanted to go back to the way I was before that morning, but I'd later realize I needed to move forward rather than backward. I texted my friend Katie. We graduated high school together, and she loves books just as much as I do. She thought of me every time there was a court hearing and supported me immensely in writing this memoir.

Katie, I need to be real with someone.

What's up? She replied to my text.

I need to stop drinking so much. I haven't really told anyone. I don't get drunk, but I'm drinking every day. It's not me. I don't know how to stop, I admitted. Maybe one to three beers a night wasn't much to some people, but to me it was.

Dano, she replied using the nickname my sister gave me when we were toddlers, *you got this. Read those books I sent you instead,* she offered. I knew I could be honest with her, and she'd give honest feedback. I tried her suggestions to not have an unhealthy vice, but I couldn't. The wounds were too fresh, I was alone, and the chaos was too loud. I continued to take the edge off, day after day.

I had to talk about the real-life problems I had been having, but because of my shame and denial, this was one thing I never admitted to anyone else. I knew it was leading me down an unhealthy path and I needed to start addressing my bad behaviors. But having a couple of drinks was like being outside in the midst of a tornado then jumping into a pool, weightlessly sinking to the bottom. It was like relieving the tension in my limbs and my body, muting my troubles, holding my breath, looking up, watching the tornado above through the water, quietly, calmly, peacefully... knowing the loudest possible thing that could be happening was right above my head. It put me in a zone of quiet fog. I was just deep enough under the water to take the edge off.

It wouldn't be until New Year's Day of 2021 that I would finally take back this control—take back my power.

14

When I woke up on Monday, March 4, 2019, I anticipated it being just another day. It was another Monday at work, and just about a week and a half until I got to close on selling my house and buying a new one. Until I read my email.

My lender from the bank I was going to use sent me a note saying he was unable to service the loan under the Safe at Home Program and I should call him to discuss. The Safe at Home Program was the program I enrolled in through the Secretary of State to make my home address confidential. I immediately called the lender and became confused and upset at why this was a problem *now*, less than two weeks to closing. He forwarded me another email saying the program director from the Safe at Home program suggested we can't follow through with the loan. I called the program director and ran through what the email said from my lender. She stated there must have been a misunderstanding because things on her end were fine. I called the lender back to relay what the program director said, and he gave me a few *different* reasons for why they couldn't service the loan but offered that he *could* service the loan if I did not use the Safe at Home Program. This was *not* an option I could consider. My credit score was 820, couldn't that make up for anything?

I WAS STILL in the thick of dealing with this loan crisis on the following day, three and a half months after the assault, when I received a text message from Investigator Dungy. I had gotten my old iPhone back from evidence and switched my burner phone number over. Dungy asked if I was working that day and if I had time to meet with him and Investigator Loken. I replied I could make anything work—thanks to my very understanding boss. He suggested we meet at the safe house. This was unusual because he usually met me wherever I was at the time, like work.

I had a lot of anxiety and anticipation about meeting with the investigators. I arranged for my mom to pick up James and planned to leave work thirty minutes early to meet with them. As I was leaving, they messaged me saying they were already in the area and to let them know when I arrived. *Red flag... what's going on?*

Staying within the speed limit, I drove as fast as I could and sent them a text letting them know when I got there. They replied saying they would be over shortly.

As I was waiting, I needed a distraction. I couldn't handle the anxiety, so I washed the dishes, turned on the fireplace, and picked up some of James's toys. Time was dragging, but only a few minutes later there was a knock at my door. I shut off my security system and greeted Investigators Dungy and Loken. We made small talk and I filled them in on how the bank suddenly pulled out from giving me a loan and how I was frustrated with the whole situation.

When the conversation came to a pause, we sat down at the table. It was a beautiful wooden table, on perfect wooden floors, with sun beaming through the patio door illuminating the kitchen. Dungy did not pull out his yellow notepad or his black binder, nor did he have his recorder out. Again, this was unusual.

"The reason we are here and wanted to talk to you in person is because we wanted to let you know we've made an arrest," Dungy stated.

My hands went up to my cheeks like Maccaulay Culkin in *Home Alone*. I was speechless. My stomach fell to the floor, and I couldn't find words.

"We arrested Jesse Anderson last night," he went on.

"What? *What?* What? Are you sure? Are you sure!?" I questioned, mortified.

Investigator Loken added, "We know without a doubt that it was Jesse." She was always calm, cool, and collected.

I became hysterical for a moment, crying and releasing the three and a half months of fear I had been bottling up. My face was in my hands, and I was slumped over with my head by my knees. Loken put her hand on my shoulder and said, "Danielle, the person that did this to you is behind bars."

When I regained my composure, I still couldn't believe it. It wasn't processing; I couldn't wrap my head around it. But at the same time, it all made sense. His height, his build, his nose, and the fact that he's told me stories about using meth in the past. And he had been "waiting for years to be in this position." It all added up to Jesse, the man I had known for eight years because he was friends with my ex-husband.

The investigators explained that Jesse was being charged with allegedly sexually assaulting a vulnerable adult who was living in a group home. It was a completely different scenario and not as violent, but it happened in Willmar, Minnesota at a group home Jesse worked at part-time. They collected DNA from Jesse because he was the suspect in that case, which in turn matched the DNA from my case. They said they had a window of opportunity to arrest him, so they went for it.

Investigators got a warrant to search his home and found boots that matched the footprints in the snow outside my house, and gloves that matched a glove print. His wife was at the house when they did the search, along with a couple of his five kids. Jesse had three kids with his first wife, and two with his second wife.

Investigator Dungy pulled out his recorder and said, "I'm going to show you a picture of something. I want you to tell me if you recognize what it is."

I replied before even seeing the photo. "Is it my green shorts?"

He pulled out a photograph of a zip lock bag that appeared to be sitting on the floor of a truck. It was next to an empty Gatorade bottle. The bag contained something green; a specific color of green I recognized as what used to be my favorite green shorts.

"Those are my shorts. If you take them out of that bag you will see there is underwear built into the shorts, there is no drawstring, and there is a small gray paint stain on the back," I replied. He must have kept them as a prize, a token, a souvenir from what he had done to me.

The investigators went on to tell me that during their interrogation of him, he basically confessed. They said he wouldn't be able to backpedal on what he'd already admitted. He admitted to being in my home and gave them details he wouldn't have known if he hadn't been there. They didn't tell me specifics and I was too overwhelmed to ask. They also noted his wife drives a maroon vehicle like the one that was seen by my house on the nights of November 16 and 17.

The fact that the DNA from my body and the guns matched Jesse's DNA made me hopeful, but I also gained a new fear. Now that he knew I told the police after he threatened me for five hours not to, he would certainly kill me if he got the chance.

"We had an officer go into the youth wrestling match where Jesse was. They got him to come outside of the building and that is when they made the arrest," Investigator Dungy told me. "He stayed in Kandiyohi County jail and we interviewed him the next morning. After that, he was transported to Winona County jail."

"He's here? He's down here? Down in southeast Minnesota?" I was petrified. I was more afraid now knowing who it was and where he was jailed than moments before, when the suspect was still unknown.

"He's behind bars, Danielle. He's in jail." Investigator Loken said. When I ran out of questions and they ran out of details to share, Dungy and Loken asked if they could wait with me until someone else came to be with me. I called Cody and he didn't hesitate to come.

"I'll call Erin..." I said nervously. I was afraid to tell her; I didn't want to speak the words. I felt so much shame that I was afraid I would lose it on the phone with her. "Would you be able to tell her, Kate?"

"Yeah, of course," she agreed.

I called my sister and thankfully she was available to answer. I asked, "Are you alone?"

"Hey. Yeah, what's up?" she asked. I handed the phone to Investigator Loken.

"Hey, Erin. It's Kate. Yeah, so we made an arrest," she told my sister. She stepped into the other room and I zoned her out because I didn't want to hear it again. Instead, I went to the fridge to grab a beer; Corona would do the trick.

ABOUT AN HOUR LATER CODY ARRIVED. He came into the safe house and asked, "What's going on?" But I couldn't find the words. I asked Dungy and Loken to fill him in. As expected, he did not take it well. Cody attended the same high school as

Jesse, he grew up with him, he worked for him, and he was a groomsman in our wedding. Cody's jaw was clenched, and his fists were like rocks. I could see the anger coursing through his forearm veins.

Cody said to me, "I should have listened to you sooner."

I had questioned if he thought it was Jesse a couple of months prior. I brought this up to him and my family, and they replied with comments like, "It's probably not him. He lives so far away. It's probably someone from down here."

At the beginning of the new year, before I knew there was meth in my system and narrowed the suspect list down considerably, I had asked Cody if he knew what Jesse's wife drove. He didn't know, so I asked him if he could find out. He wasn't sure how he could do this without being obvious so we both let it go rather than risking opening a can of worms. Cody hadn't discussed what happened to me with anyone from his hometown, Spicer, Minnesota, with exception of his mom and stepdad. Cody's theory was that it wasn't his story to tell anyway. I do trust his judgement, and in this case he sure as hell made the right call by not talking to his friends about it.

Investigators Dungy and Loken left as I was finishing my second Corona. Cody and I drove to the local bar and grill for dinner and another beer. I could go in public without the fear of wondering if the rapist was watching me because now he was behind bars. But I was still scared. Cody and I talked about what the investigators told us. I wished I could ask Cody to stay with me, but I knew I shouldn't. I pulled strength out from somewhere deep within, determined to be fine alone.

I SPENT that whole night panicking, thinking about how my attacker was just down the road in the next county to the east, sitting in a jail cell cursing my name. This was one of the many reasons I did not sleep that night. One comment I will never forget from that evening was what Jesse told his wife. Per Investigator Dungy, Jesse had told his wife he was going on a hunting trip down to Rochester that weekend. I guess that part was true... he successfully hunted me.

I was a hostage in my own home for five hours. Who knows how long it would have been if the sun wasn't coming up or if I didn't have James that night? Jesse drove nearly four hours to my house to break in and rape me. Not just the girl next door, or a girl in the same town he was in–he planned this. He knew where he was going and what he was going to do. It was premeditated. He somehow figured out where I lived. Cody and I moved from Paynesville to St. Charles a year and a half prior and we hadn't told him our address simply because we hadn't been in touch with him. He hunted me down. How long had he been staking out my house? He was the predator; I was the prey. It was a game for him. And he came fully prepared with drugs, a flashlight, zip ties, and a handgun—for hunting? I was a small-town girl; I knew better than that.

Why didn't Jesse's wife question why he was taking her SUV on a hunting trip during deer season? What was he going to do if he had shot a deer, put it in their family SUV? Why didn't she realize he was up to something? Why wouldn't he have taken his truck? Had he come down again since the assault? Had he gone on another "hunting trip" to finish me off only to find I didn't live in St. Charles anymore? It must have been obvious... I was off social media. My house was a vacant, dark, empty shelter from the snow when it wasn't filled with people collecting evidence. Then it was put up for sale and listed on the market. It would have been easy for Jesse to see my house for sale online.

What about his kids? His wife is gorgeous, why would he need to do this? What if he gets out? I was glad to be hiding in a safe house where only a few people knew where I was staying. I was thankful to have a security system installed and to be sleeping on the second floor. But despite all of this, I was petrified. How did I not know? How did he disguise his voice so well?

I'm in awe of the bravery of the vulnerable adult who reported Jesse. It couldn't have been an easy thing to do considering the factors, but I am forever grateful he did. If it had gone unreported, would he still be an unknown rapist?

15

I took Wednesday and Thursday off work to try to process the news. There was no way I would be able to focus on work. There was a live news release on the Winona County Facebook page the day after his arrest. I saw his wife's name pop up as she logged on to watch. I saw his brother and his whole family watching and waiting to hear what he did. I wondered what they were thinking and if they knew I was the victim. I didn't know many details about how his family reacted to the news. All I knew was a family member of his texted Cody, *What did that asshole do?*

If there was meth in my system at the time of the assault, he was probably on meth himself. I also found out he was allegedly robbing customers he did flooring work for and even breaking into his neighbors' homes. That was only gossip... until they found the large tote he stashed in his garage with stolen electronics in it.

News stories from Winona, Rochester, the Twin Cities, Duluth, and Willmar, Minnesota shared articles with information I hadn't heard about yet. They were getting a lot of it right, but some of it was in backwards order. Some of them had details of what Jesse said in his interview; these were things I didn't even know about yet. I wanted to know what the world knew through reading the articles. I didn't want to be left in the dark about anything. Being in the light was healing for me. One of the news articles stated Jesse said what happened was *my* idea. Just to be clear, persuading a victim to perform sex while holding a gun, threatening to kill the victim and her child is *not* consensual. It is coercion. It is rape.

Cody was getting Facebook messages and text messages from friends in Spicer. I was the only person they knew in St. Charles that could have known Jesse as well, so I guess they had connected the dots on their own. A few of our friends from Spicer told Cody to tell me they were thinking of me and to let them know if we needed anything. There were also some that supposedly mentioned he was safer in jail where they couldn't get to him. These were people from his hometown—his friends, his acquaintances. Having their support validated how I had been feeling, even more afraid upon finding out who the rapist was. It was proof they knew what kind of person he was and what he was capable of. I felt less alone having an army of people behind me.

AT JESSE'S first brief court appearance, they determined bail would be set at $1,000,000. One million dollars. I didn't know what I would do if he somehow made bail. I also didn't know the difference between conditional and unconditional bail. Turns out, he would have to post all one-million dollars to get out. I began adding things up in my head. *If they sold his house and his truck, would that be enough money? Would they get a loan?* I *had to* know if he could get out. I had to be prepared. If he could, certainly there would be other clinics in other states that would hire me as a nurse... I would move, run, hide. I'd tuck my tail between my legs and get the hell out of Minnesota with James because I knew for damn sure he would come after me.

The court appearance was at eleven a.m. on March 6. When it was his turn to speak, the judge warned him not to talk about the case as he was not represented by a lawyer yet. The first thing he said was, "I'm not denying that I went into her home," and I was relieved to hear it was all recorded. His next court appearance wouldn't be until March 20.

MEANWHILE, I was still trying to figure out my home loan situation. My mom called the bank, and they told her the issue I was having might have something to do with my pending divorce, which was never mentioned to me. Besides, if they were willing to give me the loan without using the Safe at Home Program, why would my divorce have anything to do with it?

It was time to find a new lender. But I had questions. Could they do that? Was that legal? I was infuriated. Ultimately, my opinion was they didn't want to be liable if my address was accidentally released.

One of the investigators provided me with contact information for a program called Standpoint. They have victim advocates and attorneys on staff to help women, so I called and left a message. An advocate discussed the situation with an attorney, and they determined the safest thing for me to do would be to get a new lender, rather than "forcing" this bank to service me with a loan. I was glad to have a second opinion, but it wasn't what I wanted to hear.

Within a few days I found a new lender that honored the Safe at Home Program. This pushed my closing date out a few weeks, causing issues with the sellers because of the purchase of their next house. It was a domino effect and I felt personally responsible. I hated to cause issues in other people's lives because of my situation. But eventually, after redoing all of the paperwork for a new lender, it worked out.

I returned to work Friday, March 8. It was challenging being excited about having my own home again but not being able to talk about it. I didn't want to talk about it because I didn't want to be asked why I moved and where I moved to. Being asked these questions caught me off guard and I never knew what to say. How could I tell my coworkers, "Um, yeah I bought a new house, but I can't tell you where it is."

I didn't want to lie, so I kept it vague. I also made a list of every single person that knew where I was moving to . . . just in case.

I KNEW Jesse had been accused of sexually assaulting someone from the Willmar, Minnesota area, but I wasn't sure of details and charges until my close friend pointed out new charges on the Winona County Jail roster.

The charges were listed for my case, but at the bottom listed two new charges. It said, "Criminal Sex Conduct – 3rd Degree – Victim Mental," and "Crim Abuse – Sexual – Caregiver/Staff – Vulnerable." My mind was swirling. The group home he worked at was for males. I wondered how long he had been working there and how long this could have been going on, or was it a one-time thing?

Another friend later pointed out an article that described the assault in Willmar. The West Central Tribune stated Jesse was talking to the vulnerable adult about his sex life while he was working on Christmas Day. The victim stated he had never had sex. Jesse supposedly started showing him pornography and allegedly pulled down the man's pants and assaulted him. To me, this information was further proof he was a monster and needed to be put away for a long, long time.

When I left work after that first day back, I realized I hadn't talked to my family at all that day. I needed someone to ask how I was doing, and I felt like no one cared. At the time, my mom was uncomfortable to be around because it seemed like her stress level was out of control. That wasn't something I wanted to deal with at the time, so I never reached out to her.

I called my best friend Jordan who talked some sense into me before I reached out to Cody and my mom about how I was feeling. Everyone had someone, and on that Friday night I didn't have my son, or anyone. I didn't have the one person I was *always* strong for: James. He was with his dad, and since I didn't have to be strong for him, I wasn't. I was alone. I was scared and falling quickly. I knew I should have been around people, even if they were strangers, so I went to the Crooked Pint in Rochester.

While I was there, I let my mom, Cody, and my sister know I felt alone. I told my mom and Cody I thought they needed to get their emotions in check, selfishly, so I would have someone to talk to. I wanted them to give a damn about how I was feeling. Looking back, I'm sure they did. I just *felt* alone. I can't say I was being rational. Honestly, I went to the restaurant by myself that night to sit alone surrounded by strangers who might ask me how I was doing. They didn't. I now know that if I could have networked with other survivors sooner after the assault, I would have been far better off. But instead, I sat in a bar alone, tears washing off my mascara while I wondered why no one cared and why I was going through this alone. My emotions were on a rollercoaster of anger and sadness. I was raging one moment and wondering why I was even on this earth the next. Reason number thirty-four being single sucked. The first thirty-three reasons are related to being an easier target for sexual predators.

I think what made me the most upset was something that had been happening since day one. I would reach out to my family and they would interrupt conversation and say, "You should see someone," like a counselor or psychologist. I understood I *should* see someone on a regular basis, but I felt like they didn't want to listen to me and wanted to put it on someone else. It hurt. I see now that they were just trying to help. But every time it happened, I became more upset. There's a difference between talking to a therapist and your family. I needed both.

I had already gone to talk to someone ... but only twice. The psychologist did not worry about my mental stability and after seeing her twice, she said, "Well, how about you just call if you need to?"

I wanted Erin back home from Kuwait so we could watch *Pretty Woman* or *A Cinderella Story*. I wanted to sit on the couch together where I could feel safe and loved and supported and we could spend hours sipping on beer, eating Dotz pretzels and Hot Tamales, watching shows from our past that would bring back happy, innocent memories. I went back to the safe house upon leaving Crooked Pint, opened my gun safe (a Christmas gift from my parents) and checked the gun I had bought from my dad. I checked the windows and locks, checked the basement, set the alarm, and went to bed. Alone. Being irrational only made me lonelier.

On March 13 and 14, the snow from the blizzard in February melted and the state flooded. Streets flooded and roads were shut down because they were hidden beneath pools of water. Basements flooded and material items were damaged. But on March 19 the sun came out. The air warmed and led into a beautiful first day of spring on March 20.

Despite everything, the sun would still shine.

16

THE NEXT WEEK, JAMES AND I SPENT AN ENTIRE DAY PLAYING together. I tucked him into bed, and we read a few books. I was having him sleep in my bed because his bedroom was too far down the hallway for my liking. I needed to keep him safe. The bedtime routine had grown to become longer and longer, so I tried to be prepared ahead of time. I got him a fresh glass of ice water and made sure he had all his stuffed animals and his blankie before I left the room. But as soon as I left, he yelled for me to come back.

"Mommy!"

"Yeah, buddy?"

"Will you lay with me?" he asked with those darling brown eyes gazing at me.

I stayed with him for a few minutes, gave him another good-night kiss, and as I was leaving the room, he yelled for me to stay with him again.

It wasn't unusual for him to make excuses to stay awake longer. "Mommy, can I watch cartoons?"

"Nope, time for bed, honey."

I started walking down the hallway when I heard, "Mommy!"

After close to an hour of struggling with him in and out of bed, coming out for this or that and continually wanting me in there with him, I decided to call Cody. James was upset when I got him on the phone. He was silently kicking and didn't want to talk to either of us.

"Hey, bud. What's going on? You have to listen to Mommy, okay? It's time for bed."

Finally, James said, "I don't like laying down. I don't like laying down alone," which led us to figure out he was scared.

"What are you scared of, bud?" Cody asked.

"I'm scared of the bad guy. I'm scared of the bad guy who was fixing our shower while mommy and I were watching shows in my bed," he admitted.

My heart pounded with pain and tears welled in my eyes. All I could do was grab James and hold him close. His sweet, innocent little voice he was once trying to hide was now strong but frightened.

How could I not have known? Why didn't he say so in the first place? I became instantly angry at Jesse, blaming him for everything.

"No, no. The bad guy is in jail, bud. The police are watching over him there," Cody explained.

"But what if he gets out? What if he sneaks out and he will come to our house and find us?" James challenged.

I have the same concerns, Little Man.

There was a solid ten minutes of back-and-forth between James and his dad while I was trying to hold myself together and rocking him at the same time. *I hate Jesse. I hate him. I hate him so much!*

We reviewed all the reasons why we were safe now, and that mommy and daddy will always protect him. Finally we convinced him to think about something else. I sang him a few songs and scratched his back until he could hardly keep his eyes open. I left the room to gather my things and was relieved he was sleeping when I came back. *I'm right here, my sweet boy.*

AFTER THE ARREST, I did a lot of thinking about the past. I thought about every red flag Jesse threw out there and they all made sense. I've tried to break everything down to better understand why this happened to me. The ultimate question: *Why ME?* Why did he hunt *ME* down? Why did he say, "I've been waiting for years to be in this position."? I'll probably never know the truth, but I've come up with a few theories as to why he may have picked me...

1. **Vulnerability.** I was recently separated. My dog had just died a couple of months prior. (Yes, I had put this on Facebook). My roommate had just moved out. I was alone in the house with the exception of my son. He knew the city I lived in. He must have simply Googled my address because I had never told him in the past. Cody told me about the last time he and Jesse spoke. Jesse had called Cody in the summer of 2018 to make small talk. (Note, Jesse and Cody hadn't talked much since Jesse's second wedding in 2016... he never called to chit chat, so this was unusual). What Jesse had asked Cody was, "So you and Dano are officially done now?" And Cody replied that we were... *Had he been planning this the entire time? Since the summer of 2018?*

2. **Personality.** I was nice, quiet, shy, and passive. I say, "was" rather than "am" because I've been doing things to try to get me away from the "girl-next-door" assumption. I *am* nice, but now I'm not quiet,

and I'm not passive. Jesse knew I would do what he wanted at the time. He thought I would keep quiet. He saw how loyal I was to Cody and thought I would be the same to an armed masked man. He didn't think I would put up a fight. He knew how well I took care of Cody when we were together. He knew I was a good person. Did that draw him to me? Being a decent human being?

3. **Superficial qualities.** I had done modeling in the past and was in a few advertisements. I worked out, ate healthy, was in shape and took care of myself. I liked to look nice and cared about my appearance.

4. **Retaliation.** He was angry at me because I was honest with his ex-wife about details of his "work trips" he had gone on with Cody in the past.

AND HERE I was yet again.... Trying to figure out how it was my fault.

17

MY MOM HAD BEEN ACTING ABNORMAL FOR THE LAST COUPLE OF months; we weren't talking nearly as much as we used to. I didn't know at the time she was going through the stages of grieving as well. I called her on the way to my car after work one day. She got short and stern with me and I snapped.

"Mom! Why are you being like this? No one wants to be around you when you're so crabby and angry! I didn't do anything to you!" I yelled. I told her how I felt but it did not go over well. Our conversation ended and we didn't speak again until the following week when we all had dinner with my sister.

ERIN HAD FINALLY COMPLETED her mission and was back in the United States from Kuwait, so I had something to look forward to. She was in Texas for a short time prior to her return to Minnesota. I made plans to go to lunch with Jake at the new Buffalo Wild Wings in Rochester on March 13. Jake and I were becoming closer friends as time went on. I knew Erin was on her way to town, so I told her where we were going knowing Jake would be happy to see her too.

Jake was telling me stories about how he and Erin had become like brother and sister during their time together in the military. I was lost in his story when I felt arms wrap around my shoulders and I saw the army green and tan of Erin's uniform.

"Erin!" My sister was home! I wasn't afraid of the surprise because I knew it was her and I was ecstatic she was there. I turned and stood, instantly hugging her as tight as I could. My hero was finally there with me.

"I'm so glad you're here!" I said.

"Me too," she replied, embracing me with a year's worth of hugs.

LATER THAT NIGHT, Erin, Mom and I went to Applebee's. My mom and I had things to talk about because our relationship had been especially strained since our heated conversation the week prior. Unfortunately, my sister's welcome home dinner was filled with a lot of tension. Dinner went okay and finally I said to my mom, "I'm sorry I didn't talk to you about things sooner." I hadn't told my mom everything I knew about the investigation. I didn't tell many people, but if I did it was usually my sister, Cody, and Jake. My mom and I weren't talking so I didn't go out of my way to keep her in the loop. She inadvertently found out some of the details of the investigation before I got the chance to tell her myself.

"It's hard to keep you and Erin and Cody and Jake all up to date. I don't like talking about it once, let alone four times, so sometimes I just don't."

What I heard my mom say next was, "Have you been seeing a therapist? You really need to be talking to someone." It was the last thing I wanted to hear, and it instantly made me upset.

"Mom! That isn't what this is about! I'm not the one who has been acting angry and short with everyone." My mom got up and walked out of the restaurant. In all of my 31 years, she'd never done anything like that before.

ERIN STAYED with me in the safe house and broke down the situation in words I needed to hear. "It's not your job to fix anyone else right now, Dano," she said, validating my feelings. "You need to worry about *you*. I don't know what is going on with Mom." I will be forever grateful for my sister; it truly was what I needed at that time. And finally, I didn't feel alone. I had someone who would listen to me and reply with sincerity. It was the last thing I had patience and energy for. Hell, I didn't even have patience or energy to help *myself* heal.

"Okay... I just... I don't know what I did to make her act that way. She's been short and angry with me. I feel like no one gives a damn about how I'm feeling. When was the last time she or Cody or anyone asked me how I was doing? I can't even tell you. I have no idea," I replied. I was confused with her feelings and everyone else's feelings, on top of my own. But I later learned my mom was a secondary victim. I should have been more understanding; I had no idea at the time. Also, it wasn't their job to babysit me and my emotions every day.

Erin and I were hanging out on the couch watching TV when my dad called her. I was sitting right next to her and I heard him instantly cursing my name, screaming through the phone that I was an awful person. He said a lot of nasty words about me that I unfortunately heard sitting right next to Erin. *Lovely.*

Erin got off the phone and said, "Maybe don't talk to them for a while." *Done.*

"I have no intention to," I said. Why invite even more pain and hurt into my life than I already had?

My mom was a rock and an amazing person. She had a

heart of gold and always did what was best. She was the hardest worker I knew. That shows how challenging being a secondary victim could be. My mom and I had never *not* gotten along in the past. But now, less than 10 days after Jesse was arrested, we weren't even on speaking terms. I blame him. He made her a secondary victim. He made her go through the stages of grief. He broke us, but eventually we mended our relationship. We wouldn't let him win.

FOR THE NEXT month I suffered through attempting to heal from the assault, selling my house, buying a new house, moving, Jesse being arrested, and trying to get life back on track all without my mom and dad. Oh, and knowing that a man wanted to murder my son and me. The next time I would speak to my mom and dad was when we celebrated Erin's birthday together almost a month later.

Everything, including my losses, were piling up. When I would drive to work, I would sometimes listen to music that made me cry. But of course I would compose myself before I left my car. I walked zombie-like down the halls from the employee parking ramp (Elizabeth had been able to get me a spot!) to my department, but alert enough to be able to grab my pepper spray in an instant if I had to. I was always aware of my surroundings and had multiple defense mechanisms in place for my protection.

I'd get to my floor and sit in an empty procedure room across from my workroom with the lights still off, silently staring into the darkness. It was a moment of silence from the chaos in my traumatized mind before the chaos of the workday. When it was time, I would get up, walk across the hallway into my workroom and start my day with a smile on my face. I would be so busy that the day would fly by, and I would forget how broken I truly was. Many days I was so busy I could hardly fit a break in, but whatever would help the days go by faster would speed up the time for me to get to ...what? Happiness? Trial? "Getting over" this?

There was no getting over it.

18

ON MARCH 20, 2019, JESSE HAD ANOTHER COURT APPEARANCE. He was represented by a defense attorney this time. The prosecutors were there (who I still hadn't met nor spoken to) along with investigators from the case. I was told bail was going to be re-discussed. The defense attorney was going to request bail be lowered.

Bail was going to be re-discussed. This made me sick to my stomach. Lowering bail would raise the chances of him being able to get out, and I knew what would be on his mind when he did: hunting me again.

I was pacing around until I finally got a text from Investigator Loken, "I'm at the courthouse. Just waiting for the hearing to start." I paced for another hour until I heard back.

A man from the Women's Resource Center (WRC) in Winona called and filled me in on how court went. It was someone I hadn't spoken to before, but I was reassured knowing he was from the WRC.

"Bail stands at $1,000,000 unconditionally. The next court appearance is May 1st at 9:00 am," he said. I felt some relief. *I don't need to move out of state and find a new job.*

"Do I need to go to the next court date?" I asked anxiously.

"No. You are not required to go, but you can if you want to. Do you have any other questions?"

"No. But thank you."

After we hung up, Investigator Loken called and filled me in on a few more things.

"The defense attorney requested bail to be set at $25,000. Jesse looked hopeful bail would be lowered."

"What did his face look like when he found out it wasn't going to be lowered?" I asked.

"He didn't turn around even once. But he shook his head in disbelief." *Good.*

I hated that I wouldn't tell my parents what happened at court because we still weren't speaking, but I planned to tell Erin and she'd probably fill them in.

WORD on the street was that Jesse's wife was pregnant. There was also a rumor Jesse had installed cameras in his sister-in-law's bathroom and bedroom and had footage from them. Even more charges piled up for him. *That could only help and extend his jail sentence, right?* I hoped. But I clearly didn't understand the law.

19

MARCH 29, 2019 WAS THE NIGHT I TOOK CARE OF MY OLD mattress. Earlier in the year, before my mom and I were on such bad terms, we'd brought my mattress out to my friend Leah's house to store until there was a good evening—blizzard-free—to burn it.

Now that the weather was decent for a fire, Leah and her husband asked if I wanted to use the tainted mattress for target practice with an automatic rifle (AR) before we burned it.

Hell. Yes.

Erin and I went to their house where Leah watched my son with her kids while we went down the hill to the mattress. Her husband and his friend Josh were down there ready to go. Josh had his AR loaded and they had set the mattress up for me to shoot.

I put the noise-canceling headphones over my stocking cap, anxious for the hands-on therapy session I was about to have. I had been waiting four and a half months for this. I settled the AR into my right shoulder and raised the gun. I turned off the safety and loaded a round. I aimed in the center of the mattress and shot.

And shot, and shot, and shot.

And when the clip was empty, I checked my work as the boys and my sister, an excellent shot in the military, said, "Wow! Nice grouping!"

I took the two red gas cans the guys had brought down and dumped gas on the mattress, every last drop. They made a small trail of gas for me from the fire pit to where we were standing. I took the lighter, bent down, and lit the trail of gas.

Within a second, the ground lit on fire and traveled to the pile where the mattress sat on top. The whole thing lit up in flames as if the fire had emerged from a volcano inside the earth to swallow the mattress whole. And it felt so good.

Isn't that what you said when you pulled out? It felt so fucking good? Yeah, so did this, Mother Fucker.

AT THE END of March I moved into my new home with help from my sister and a few friends. We moved everything out of the storage units and got things put together in my house. The one room that was particularly bare was my bedroom. I had my clothes in the closet, and that's about it.

My boss Jenny knew I didn't have anything to sleep on and made connections with friends at work. The next thing I knew, a resident I work with, Dr. Derek Gearman, was offering me one of his spare beds because he was going to be moving in the next couple of months and didn't need to take it with him. *...Really!?*

Part of me would rather have slept on the floor than accept charity, but at the same time, if James wanted to crawl in bed with me because he was scared, I didn't want him to have to sleep on the floor. I accepted the bed and thanked him for his kindness and generosity. The bed was barely used, it came with a frame, and oh my, it was sure comfortable. He also offered a dresser he didn't need since I had left mine at my St. Charles home.

Anne, Tessa, and Cara (my amazing co-workers) graciously found me sheets, pillows, a blanket, and a beautiful burgundy comforter for my new bed. It felt good to have an untainted bed to sleep on with fresh bedding. I slept surrounded by love from my friends. Knowing it was a place of Zen filled with peace rather than a place of crime, heartache, and PTSD, helped me fall asleep on my first night in my new home. Along with the security system that we moved from the safe house to this house, of course.

WHEN I LIVED at my old house, on those warm spring days nearing summer and at the brink of fall, I would open all the windows and let the fresh air flow through. Every chance I got, the blinds, curtains, and windows were wide open to welcome the sun, the air, and freedom.

When the sky dimmed and the sun hugged the west end of the earth, I'd close the windows and snuggle on the couch with my little man. The windows I left open were in my bedroom. Two windows, side by side. *Who doesn't love to sleep in a cool room?!*

After tucking in my little man, I would lie my head on my cool pillow, feeling the night breeze whisper through the screen and across my gray blanket, kissing my face as it passed. I'd hear the birds say their goodnights, and the crickets sing in harmony. I'd smell the fresh night air accompanied with a faint scent of smoke coming from the neighborhood as neighbors stayed out late having bonfires.

It would only take me a matter of minutes (if that) for the night to capture me and whisk me off into a deep sleep. In the morning, I would wake with the morning breeze whispering, "Good morning, sunshine," in my chilled room. It was always comforting being snuggled under the covers with the crisp morning air surrounding my face.

Ever since I moved to my new house, I knew I would never sleep with my windows open again. The master bedroom was on the main level. There was no way I could fathom or rationalize leaving the windows open while I slept. In my old house, it created peace and comfort, whereas now... There was just no way.

I *longed* for that cool breeze to lull me to sleep... I *longed* to smell the fresh air and feel the draft of freedom paint my bed at night... If only I could hear the birds and the crickets while I drifted off to sleep again... I knew I would be one step closer to (yet still miles away from) a comfort and contentment I once knew.

20

On April 4 of 2019, Investigators Dungy and Loken came to my work. When we arrived at the conference room in the security office, they had a piece of paper with them. I was nervous, much like when they had the paper claiming there was meth found on my urine test.

"We have a subpoena here," Dungy said, showing me the paper. I was being subpoenaed to testify in front of a secret grand jury to determine if additional charges could be added to the case. The significance of the charges was that they had a maximum of a life sentence, or at minimum, they would extend his sentence compared to the charges he was currently facing. To put it into perspective, the last time Winona County had a grand jury hearing was for a homicide. I guess I came out four pounds of pressure ahead; one simple trigger pull ahead of the last time there was a grand jury.

"Court will be on April 15. You'll be testifying but Jesse won't be there. It will just be the grand jury members, prosecutors, and court transcriptionist. Your mom is being subpoenaed as well." He continued, "The prosecutors will have you give your testimony. They'll ask you some questions but then the jury

members will be able to ask you questions too." This was
frightening to try to process, but truthfully, I was glad I'd be
able to answer their questions and elaborate on things they
didn't understand. But I was still afraid. What if I forgot something that happened? What if I miss something? This gave me
less than two weeks' notice until I would testify in front of
sixteen to twenty-three members of a grand jury. I didn't know
what to say. I didn't know what to ask.

ON APRIL 10 I went to Winona County to meet with the prosecutors so they could explain the procedure for the following
Monday. I learned the main prosecutor would be Christina
Galewski. Before I met with them, I met with Investigator
Dungy in his office at the jail next to the courthouse. He filled
me in on some bits of information he recently learned that he
didn't want me to have to find out from anyone else.

The bomb dropped. "I wanted you to know, before you
found out from anyone else, Jesse had recorded videos that
morning at your house," Dungy said. I knew Jesse had taken
photos off my devices, multiple photos from my cell phone, and
had stolen my old Mac computer, but I had no idea there was a
video.

I stared blankly.

What?

I was instantly humiliated and mortified. *Did I hear him
correctly?* "What?"

"He took videos while he was at your house," he elaborated,
knowing I wasn't able to process the initial bomb that was
dropped. I was violated all over again. This feeling was
happening a lot. I felt sick. I was speechless. I stared at Investigator Dungy. My insides wanted to fall out, my heart sank to the
floor, and my mind was racing. And all sixteen to twenty-three

members of the grand jury, along with the prosecutors and investigators, would probably be watching that video.

"So everything I said in my initial interview is validated with these videos," I said, but more to myself than anything. Was I supposed to feel relieved that there was more evidence? I would eventually, but at this point I was disgusted and tremendously violated.

I was alone and didn't have a choice but to keep my head up and continue on with the conversation.

"Okay... okay. So, they'll see the video?" I asked, referring to the grand jury members.

"Yeah, it will be part of the evidence presented," he explained. Not only was it evidence, but it was a trophy video he had probably watched countless times. A video that his wife would've had access to find... and she did find. But his lies and manipulation kept pulling her away from the truth, believing what he wanted her to believe.

A new anger brought a new bravery and will to fight.

Let's do this, I thought.

INVESTIGATOR DUNGY WALKED me to the courthouse. A new fire burned in my soul. A new darkness. A new shade of red.

There were three prosecutors and two other people in the conference room. Claire was a Victim Services Coordinator for the courthouse. I'd been corresponding with her via email.

The prosecutors asked me a ton of questions about the morning of November 18, 2018, in random order. "On Monday we'll go in chronological order," Ms. Galewski explained. "You will be the first person to testify. Take your time answering questions and you can take a break whenever you need. Your mom will testify after you, either that same day or the next morning."

"What if I say something I'm not supposed to? Like something about the evidence?" I asked. I didn't want to mess up.

"We will stop you from answering any questions the jury asks, if needed," Ms. Galewski explained.

When things got out of order, I felt like I was being quizzed. Thankfully, I hadn't been drunk or drugged and had a sober mind that morning. But I had to admit, remembering five-hours of horror in the exact order it happened was challenging. It also sucked to have to remember so I could retell it multiple times.

"That's all of the questions we have for you. Do you have any other questions for us?"

"No, I guess not. I just want to make sure I say everything I need to," I replied.

"You will do great. Don't hesitate to email Claire in the meantime if you have more questions, otherwise we will see you on Monday morning. Come up the first set of stairs in the courthouse and there will be a buzzer to the right. Press that and ask for Claire."

"Will do..." I said.

I'm ready; show no mercy.

WHEN I LEFT WINONA, I was alone and flooded with emotions. I kept my composure and drove to my parents' house where we celebrated Erin's birthday. I hadn't spoken to my parents in weeks, but I was more than capable of being civil for my sister's sake on her birthday.

"You got subpoenaed too?" I asked my mom.

"Yes. I'll have to talk to my work. I'll have to take off Monday in case they call me, and Tuesday too, if I don't testify Monday." Mom replied.

We celebrated Erin that night and topped it off with an ice cream cake that read, "Happy Birthday Danielle and Erin." My birthday was March 2, and we hadn't celebrated it at all, until now, I guess.

"Happy birthday, Sister," I told her.

"Happy birthday to you, Sister," she replied. There was a silent understanding that even though tension was immensely awkward between my parents and me, we all still loved each other and would try our best to get along.

It was hard going through the anticipation of the grand jury proceeding without being able to talk about it with anyone. If I did, it could have resulted in me getting a misdemeanor. The grand jury is conducted in secrecy in all cases for reasons such as if it was public, witnesses may be hesitant to come forward voluntarily, they may be hesitant to speak freely, or the indicted might flee or influence grand jurors. And the last thing I needed was a misdemeanor. I felt like a bottle rocket with a starter-string that was a half-mile long, and the anticipation and anxiety of this being over dragged on, and on and on.

21

I HAD GONE TO A LITTLE BOUTIQUE NEAR MY JOB AND ASKED FOR the owner, as suggested by my best friend Jordan. The owner helped me find clothes to wear; she even stayed late to help. She guessed my size just by glancing at me and found me a conservative black pencil skirt that had conveniently been on sale. Never thought I'd own one of those...

I stopped at Macy's in the mall to pick out a blazer. *What the hell am I looking for? I've never done this before.* I texted one of my girlfriends from high school who was now an attorney; she was able to give me some suggestions. I picked out a plain black blazer. How fitting: black like my soul; that's how it felt anyway.

On the morning of April 15, I decided on a pair of black slacks rather than the skirt, my black blazer with a gray top underneath, and black modest heels. I was ready. *Game face on.* I had to pep-talk myself because I didn't have anyone else to do it for me. Not even Jake or Cody knew what I was up to.

I dropped James off at daycare on my way to Winona then met with Claire at the courthouse. She led me to the same conference room I was in when I initially met everyone. They had suggested I bring a book, so I pulled out *Dear John* by

Nicholas Sparks and started re-reading it, hoping it would ease my mind. I crossed my ankles and leaned back in the chair while staring at the words in the book. Soon enough I was envisioning the characters and trying to be in their shoes instead of my own when suddenly there was a soft knock at the door.

"Hey there. Are you ready?" Claire asked.

I closed my book and stuffed it into my purse, "I suppose so."

Because the grand jury proceeding was secret, we had to meet in an undisclosed location. My heels clicked as I walked, and I was brought to the place I would wait until the prosecutors were ready for me.

"You can wait here. They will come to get you when they are ready for you. You'll be sitting at a table in front of the room. Do you need anything while you wait?" Claire asked.

Um, to not be here? I thought.

A moment later, Investigator Loken walked by unexpectedly.

"Hey!" I said, ecstatic to see a friendly face in addition to Claire's. I was able to make small talk with her and it instantly lifted my spirits.

"Hey, how's it going?" she asked.

"Oh you know..." I said, assuming she knew why I was there.

"So you're just waiting for them to call you in?" she asked.

"Yep... I like your new tattoo, that's awesome." I grasped onto anything I could to get my mind off of what was about to happen.

"Thank you! You're going to do great, Dano," she said.

A few minutes later, the male prosecutor came out of the room, "We're ready for you now." I took a deep breath, grabbed my purse, held my head high, and made my way in.

As I entered, I noticed the room looked like a classroom. There were rows of tables lined with twenty-two jury members, another table with three prosecutors and the court reporter. I was seated at the front of the room at a four-legged card table with a simple chair. I was glad I chose the pants so the jury wouldn't be able to see my bare legs.

I testified for three hours. Sometimes I looked at the jury members themselves, but mostly I peered at the wall in the back of the room above their heads. I was asked to speak louder... It was incredibly hard.

Since I was the first to testify, they hadn't gotten to hear from Investigator Dungy nor my mom. They hadn't been shown the evidence nor had they watched the video of me being raped—the evidence from Jesse's phone. They hadn't heard his initial statement and him admitting to being in my home. I wondered how they felt when they watched the video. I wondered what part of the night he recorded on his phone. I wondered what body parts of mine all twenty-two jury members and prosecutors saw. I wondered if they felt even a fraction of what I felt.

THREE DAYS LATER, I received a phone call from the Winona County Courthouse. Ms. Galewski said, "We wanted to let you know there is a court hearing tomorrow morning. We can't discuss details over the phone right now. We will be able to call you afterwards and fill you in if you don't attend the hearing. You aren't required to go."

"Okay. I'll be there," I replied.

It was hard not hearing the "results" right away, but I guessed that since there was going to be a court hearing, it must be good news. I had to be careful of what I said to Erin and Cody since neither knew what was going on. I called them both, letting them know there was a hearing scheduled for Friday, April 19, and I wanted them both to attend with me.

. . .

ON THE MORNING of April 19, I met Cody and we rode to Winona together. We met Erin and the investigators at the jail prior to walking over to the courthouse. I had informed Cody and Erin that Jesse had video recorded part of the assault and they were both as upset as I was.

Cody, Erin, the investigators and I walked from the Winona County Jail to the Courthouse. We waited in the lobby until just a couple of minutes before the hearing was to start. We filed in and sat in the last two rows on the far-right side. In front of me were the investigators, to my left was Cody, to my right was Erin then Claire, and an advocate from the Winona County Women's Resource Center. I was surrounded, protected from Jesse being able to see me on the off chance he looked at the audience.

My nerves were screaming. I wanted to curl up in a ball. I wanted to be covered with Harry Potter's invisibility cloak. It would be my first time seeing Jesse since that morning, at which time I had no idea of his identity. Cody's nerves seemed to be more prominent than mine. His fists were clenched, and his jaw was tight. He couldn't sit still, and his posture was in the "ready-to-attack" mode.

I first saw his dark hair and his tall stature. I saw his broad shoulders and facial hair. I saw the man in the mask, the man who raped me, the man who threatened to murder my child, the man who almost took my life. But now he was the one tied up unwillingly. He was brought in by a police officer. He sat only a handful of rows in front of us.

What happened next was something that could only be fully grasped by witnessing it in person.

Judge Leahy stated, "Mr. Anderson, the grand jury has indicted you with the following eighteen felonies:

    1. Criminal Sexual Conduct in the First Degree – Fear of Great Bodily Harm (Firearm)

2. Criminal Sexual Conduct in the First Degree – Armed with a Dangerous Weapon, Firearm
3. Criminal Sexual Conduct in the First Degree – Injury – Use of Force/Coerce
4. Criminal Sexual Conduct in the Second Degree – Personal Injury – Force/Coerce
5. Criminal Sexual Conduct in the Second Degree – Personal Injury – Mental Impairment
6. Criminal Sexual Conduct in the First Degree – Penetration – Fear of Great Bodily Harm
7. Criminal Sexual Conduct in the First Degree – Penetration – Armed with Dangerous Weapon – Firearm
8. Criminal Sexual Conduct in the First Degree – Penetration – Injury – Force/Coerce
9. Criminal Sexual Conduct in the Second Degree – Personal Injury – Force/Coerce
10. Criminal Sexual Conduct in the Second Degree – Personal Injury – Mental Impairment
11. Criminal Sexual Conduct in the First Degree – Fear of Great Bodily Harm
12. Criminal Sexual Conduct in the First Degree – Armed with Dangerous Weapon
13. Criminal Sexual Conduct in the First Degree – Penetration – Injury/Coerce
14. Criminal Sexual Conduct in the Second Degree – Personal Injury – Force/Coerce
15. Criminal Sexual Conduct in the First Degree – Personal Injury – Mental Impairment
16. Burglary in the First Degree – Dangerous Weapon
17. Burglary in the First Degree – Occupied Dwelling
18. Burglary in the First Degree – Assault Person in Building

THEY AGREED to indict him on additional charges. Over half of the felonies had a maximum of a life sentence in prison. His bail would raise to $2 million, as the judge said he was even more of a flight risk with the additional charges. I couldn't imagine what Cody and my sister were thinking. They still probably didn't understand what was happening.

AFTER THE HEARING, we gathered in a private conference room to talk.

"I had to testify in front of a grand jury on Monday. The prosecutors had me tell the story and they asked me questions but then the jurors got to ask me questions too. I had to talk loud enough for everyone to be able to hear me. That part sucked," I explained.

"Oh, wow," was all Erin seemed to be able to say.

"Mom testified too..." I continued.

"Yeah, I suppose. That makes sense," Cody chimed in.

Claire explained the legal aspect of things, "If he's convicted of these charges in a jury trial, he will get a longer sentence. The only charge previously had a maximum of 12 years in prison, which he would only have to serve two-thirds of due to the Good Time Served rule. He's facing more prison time now." Claire was excellent at explaining things to us and putting them in layman's terms.

She went on, "The purpose of the grand jury is to determine the charges. Ethically, grand juries are convened when the max penalty for a charge is life in prison. They prevent one prosecutor from making that decision and bringing forward a charge with a max penalty of life in prison."

. . .

Cody, Erin, and I got ourselves some lunch and a celebratory beer. My mom couldn't get time off work to come with, but I was happy Erin and Cody came with me that day. The beer went down like water and helped to calm some of the tension I felt. It was certainly something that wouldn't have meant as much if I had tried to explain it to them over the phone. So, there we were, ready for the next step. But unfortunately it would be months before the case made any real progress.

Winona County grand jury indicts man who allegedly raped St. Charles woman at gunpoint
Madeline Heim and Tobias Mann Winona Daily News – Apr 19, 2019

A 30-year-old Spicer, Minn., man accused of raping a St. Charles woman at gunpoint in November was indicted by a Winona County grand jury Friday on eight counts of criminal sexual conduct and burglary in the first degree.

Jesse Taylor Anderson was previously charged by criminal complaint with seven offenses, which have held him in custody on a $1 million bond since March 6. Friday he was indicted on five counts of first and second-degree criminal sexual conduct, as well as three counts of first-degree burglary.

Anderson's bail will be set at $2 million without conditions before his next court appearance, April 24 at 9 a.m. at the Winona County Courthouse. The criminal sexual conduct charges all carry the possibility of life imprisonment without the chance for release.

. . .

I<small>N</small> M<small>INNESOTA</small>, crimes punishable by life imprisonment can only be issued upon indictment by a grand jury, according to a press release sent Friday by Winona County Attorney Karin Sonneman.

A<small>CCORDING</small> <small>TO</small> <small>THE</small> <small>CRIMINAL</small> <small>COMPLAINT</small>, the burglary and assault began around 1 am on Nov. 18, 2018, lasting until around 6 a.m. However, the attack wasn't immediately reported to the St. Charles Police Department because the woman feared for her child's safety.

T<small>HE</small> <small>WOMAN</small> <small>TOLD</small> investigators that on Nov. 18, she woke to discover a masked man wielding a handgun—now identified by DNA analysis as Anderson—standing in her bedroom.

A<small>NDERSON</small> <small>REPORTEDLY</small> <small>TIED</small> the woman up before proceeding to rape her three times over the course of five hours.

T<small>HE</small> <small>WOMAN</small> <small>REPORTED</small> that Anderson made repeated threats of violence toward her and her child if she didn't cooperate, at one point saying he was a "rapist, not a monster," the criminal complaint said.

T<small>HE</small> <small>WOMAN</small> <small>TOLD</small> police that during the third assault Anderson held a gun to her face.

P<small>RIOR</small> <small>TO</small> <small>LEAVING</small>, Anderson reportedly attempted to disable the woman's telephone and destroy any evidence of his being there.

·   ·   ·

ACCORDING TO THE CRIMINAL COMPLAINT, Anderson threatened to kill her child if she reported the assaults to police.

THE EXTENSIVE INVESTIGATION that followed involved several law enforcement agencies including the St. Charles Police Department, the Winona County Sheriff's Office, the Winona City Police Department, the Kandiyohi County Sheriff's Office and the Minnesota Bureau of Criminal Apprehension.

22

I WAS NOT GETTING THE TIME I NEEDED TO PROCESS AND HEAL. Between working full time, trying to keep somewhat of a social life so my friends wouldn't forget about me, being a single mom, and a home-owner, there wasn't much time left for myself to do the things that facilitated healing. When I *did* find time to do something I enjoyed, like writing, I would completely indulge and savor every minute of it.

I started going to a sexual assault survivor support group on April 22. I'll be honest; it took some convincing to get me to go. I talked about it with family and friends, and they thought it would be good for me to attend and network. It turned out to be one of the best decisions I made.

The first group meeting went great, as did the second. Everyone was nice and most of us were shy, scared, and hesitant to be there. The two hosts that facilitated and led the group were beyond phenomenal. They were excellent resources and demonstrated professionalism while providing expert opinions and advice. There was a silent but strong mutual respect amongst the group. It was a deep connection we felt having gone through similar situations.

At the second meeting, I brought up an episode of *Grey's Anatomy* I'd watched when I was living in the safe house, before I moved into my new home. In the episode, one of the doctors, Jo, learned she was the product of a rape. Her mother gave her up for adoption days after she was born because all she could see was the rapist when she looked at Jo. Another story in the episode was about a woman who came into the hospital with concerning bruises and marks on her body. The woman later admitted to being raped but didn't want to report it nor tell her husband. She was afraid her rape kit would sit in a box somewhere and nothing would be done about it anyway. It turned out that the woman needed emergency surgery and as she was wheeled down the hallway on the hospital bed, the walls were lined with women (patients and staff) showing their support and protection for her. The survivor ended up reporting the assault to the police. Jo, the doctor, ended up struggling immensely with realizing she was product of a rape.

I sat on the floor in the hallway of that beautiful home watching the episode crying alone in the darkness. The only light was a dim glow from my laptop reflecting on the tears streaming down my face. I was a mess when it showed women lining the hallway for her. I was glad to see Shonda Rhimes put something so real and raw in her show.

Yeah, it was a trigger for me. Yeah, it sucked to watch alone (James was with his dad). Yeah, I sobbed. But I tell you what: everyone needs to know. Everyone needs to see it. I wish all people were supportive of survivors. I wish we were all believed. I wish rape kits didn't sit in warehouses. I wish we didn't have to fear retaliation.

In a different episode of *Grey's Anatomy*, Shonda Rhimes had one of the characters say, "There's something about experiencing the worst day of your life that is oddly freeing." This touched my soul. I replayed this scene over and over, and I sent a Snapchat of it to my sister and closest friends. While I was in a difficult place having just finished grand jury, moving into a new home, and barely speaking with my parents, I felt like I could live fuller days. I had to. I felt like I was given a second chance to live, so I better be sure to take it and live life to the fullest. I was content prior, but now it was time to start *living*.

AT THE THIRD support group meeting, we were talking about secondary victims. The discussion question was, "What are some positive and negative responses from secondary victims in your life?" This was a great topic to discuss because I learned not only what a secondary victim was, but that it can be normal for them to have significantly different responses. Unfortunately, the relationship between my mom and I was suffering because of it.

When it was my turn to talk, I talked about how Cody had stepped up a lot and how Erin had been my rock, as well as my friends, aunts and uncles, and coworkers. And out of nowhere reality struck. I needed to get something off my chest. My feelings erupted like a volcano, and I started hysterically crying and admitted, "I miss my mom." I was able to release these words in the safety of that room with people who would understand and not direct me to a therapist immediately.

"Your mom is a secondary victim in this, Danielle. She's grieving too," one of the hosts explained.

"Absolutely. She may be in an anger phase right now and sometimes they can do more damage than good," the other host elaborated. "Is your mom seeing someone?"

"Yeah, she is now," I said, remembering my sister told me she was seeing a therapist.

The group offered reassurance and validated my feelings. It was extremely difficult to regain my composure after finally verbalizing this pain of going through the worst aftermath of my life without my mom. It was an unfortunate but normal reaction my mom was having, per the hosts of the group, but it seemed like it was at my expense.

IT WAS around this time I had bought a motorcycle. My sister told me Mom felt like I was being reckless, even though I had a motorcycle in the past, and this seemed to add to our falling out. Maybe it was reckless. It was financially reckless, that's for sure. Maybe I had become a thrill-seeker. But you know what else it was? *Therapeutic.* Incredibly therapeutic. Especially because Jake, who by this point had become one of my best friends, got a motorcycle too. He credits me for him getting a motorcycle. I'll take it.

When Jake and I went riding, all that mattered was the road in front of me and the two wheels keeping me on the ground. It was escapism. I could forget about the life of mine that had completely turned upside down, leaving that life in the past and only focusing on what was right ahead of me and where I was headed. It was my place of Zen. And Jake became my ride or die.

IT WAS in support group where I learned what to prepare myself for regarding the court process. One of the girls mentioned that going to the small court hearings may be beneficial because it had helped get her used to the courtroom setting and seeing the rapist. It was a brilliant realization in addition to knowing I'd rather witness what was happening in person. I was in the dark for five hours that morning, and then again for another three and a half months until they found him. I didn't want to be in the dark anymore.

Let there be light.

June 10 would be our last support group until next fall when the hosts would coordinate another session. I couldn't wait to attend again. It was free, completely anonymous, and they would never make anyone talk if they didn't want to. I was beginning to understand the importance of connecting with people who had been sexually assaulted as well. We were validating each other and creating a strong bond. There was such a deep sense of connection in meeting with these women and they were helping to fill the void in my life that was created by Jesse. I can't imagine how lonely I would have continued to feel if I hadn't met them and started my networking journey. I wouldn't just be a few steps behind in my healing progress, I would be miles behind.

23

I HAD BEEN RECEIVING LETTERS AND PACKAGES IN THE MAIL HERE and there, particularly around court dates and special occasions, from my dear friend Katie. She's the first person I let read my journal when I realized it was turning into a book; writing a book was a dream I've had since I was a kid. Katie always gave amazing feedback. When I felt alone, she reminded me I wasn't.

May flew by and June was closing in.

The weekend prior to the June 5 court hearing, I was digging through a box in my garage looking for a lighter to start a fire in my backyard with James. We were going to have s'mores. I noticed something shiny and picked it up. I said to myself, "Oh, here are those scissors from my bathroom!"

A split second later I tossed them out of my hands onto the floor of my garage. *The scissors from that morning. The scissors he found in my bathroom and used to cut the zip ties off my wrists.*

I texted the investigators letting them know what I had found and asked if they needed them. They replied that they would mark in their file that they had been recovered, but they didn't need them at this point. I put the scissors in a plastic baggie and hid them on a shelf in my pantry. No way in hell I would be using those scissors again.

THE NEXT WEEK I had another nightmare. I had been having them since the assault, but this nightmare was particularly troubling. It was a reenactment of the assault and the guest of horror was Jesse. He was raping me again and I was trying to get away but wasn't able to escape. It was like the movie *Groundhog Day*, a never-ending repeating horror. I remember putting sharp objects in the pockets of the jeans I was wearing when I was trying to get away, like tweezers and the exact silver scissors he used to cut the zip ties off my wrists, but he would catch me every time and find the makeshift weapons. He took them away and assaulted me again. It went around and around, and I couldn't escape. When I woke up in the morning I laid in bed and stared at the ceiling. *Was that real? Where am I? What date is it? Where is James?*

I sat up and swung my feet over the edge of the bed. I put my toes in the carpet and the LED string lights around the bottom of my bed lit up my ankles. I could see every inch of my bed perimeter.

When I finally came to my senses, I realized it was only a nightmare. I felt my heart beating in my chest, pushing fresh blood cells throughout my body, reminding me I was okay. *It wasn't real,* I had to keep telling myself. But the knot in my stomach wouldn't go away for the rest of the day. It was an unease I was getting used to having after every nightmare, trigger, and episode of PTSD. It would be a reminder that despite the extremes I arranged to keep my son and I safe, *feeling safe,* could be easily ripped away from me in one small noise at the end of my bed.

But I got up and continued on with my day. I had to. It

wasn't the first nor the last nightmare I had of being repeatedly assaulted.

JUNE 5 WAS the Default Omnibus hearing. It was the same day Jenny came back to work from her three months of maternity leave. I was sad to miss her first day back, but knew it was important for me to attend the hearing.

Erin traveled all the way from the Twin Cities to the courthouse in Winona. It was almost pointless because the defense attorney asked for an extension and for the hearing to be rescheduled thirty to sixty days out. When it was, the defense requested that Jesse have access to the grand jury transcript. He also requested that a copy of the video (the video Jesse recorded on his phone of the assault) be made for the defense to keep and review. With strict court-ordered privacy restrictions, the defense attorney didn't know there was a video until a week prior to the hearing.

"Motion granted," Judge Leahy responded.

No. No...

More people to watch the video of me being raped—the most vulnerable, sensitive, awful thing that had happened to me... *lovely.*

I was bothered by this but at the same time, it was a huge win by having this evidence. I was violated and broken already, allowing more people to have access to the video was only beating the already broken soul I carried.

I HAD BEEN THINKING about getting a German Shepherd for months. If I had a protective dog last November, maybe Jesse wouldn't have been able to break into my house in the first place. What I needed was a guard dog. Despite having a security system, I needed more. What if my system failed or I forgot to set the alarm?

I had been scouring the internet trying to find an adult, trained dog that would get along with my two cats and son. It was an impossible search. Towards the beginning of the summer, Investigator Loken's wife had found the organization Firefighters with PTSD. The organization trained German Shepherds to give to first responders with PTSD.

I received a phone call from the founder, Matt Doughty, and he was so nice. "I have a perfect fit for you. We have a litter of puppies that we don't have enough trainers for so we're selling them to the public. I have one little girl I think would be perfect for your family."

"Oh, great! Thank you so much." I couldn't wait to get a guard dog.

"Since you have two cats and a kiddo, it's best you get a puppy so it can grow up with them. And I'm thinking a girl will fit your needs," Matt said.

I GOT my little pup in mid-July when she was eight weeks old. I was ready: kennel, food, a fully fenced in backyard, and dog books and magazines. Yeah, it was the start of a lot of damn work, and a new ball-and-chain, but I needed protection and I would make it work. And I did.

I named her Leona ("like a lion" in German) and she grew to be my protector. She slept at the foot of my bed, right where I needed protection. As she grew up with my son, they became best friends. She was smart and did well with him; she became his protector too.

REMEMBER the rumor from a while back? The one that Jesse had installed a secret camera in his wife's sister's house when he'd redone her bathroom for her? It turned out to be true. In July of 2019, Jesse received court paperwork from Hennepin County for these charges. They found video footage on electronics he had in a gray tote they found in his garage.

Jesse and his wife filed for divorce over the summer. She was currently pregnant with his sixth child—something I had found out from Cody back in March. Jesse had convinced his wife that he was only going to have to serve a couple of years and would be out in no time. I'm sure she and her family believed it because it was all they knew. They had two years of lies to decipher—what was true and what was not? They had no advocate, only his word.

Authorities found clothing from two other women in Jesse's possession but of course he was claiming they were consensual encounters. They hadn't been able to get ahold of one of the ladies and the other was in prison. Additional evidence supposedly showed Jesse's hacking abilities. I wasn't initially concerned to hear he stole my old white Mac computer because I had wiped it clean with intent to sell. I then found out he recovered an old video and photos of me from that computer. There was also evidence the video he stole from this old computer was shared with others at a job site. My life, my body, my most personal memories were stolen and potentially publicly shared with God knows who. There was a minor hold-up in his first appearance for this charge. They weren't sure if it should be in Winona County where he stole the files, or Kandiyohi County where he shared them. Again, I was already broken and beaten down when I found out about this – how much more hurt could there be?

As Sarah Super (another rape survivor, creator and founder of Break the Silence Day) said, *What hurt the most was that I was so happy while someone was waiting to hurt me.* It was true for me too. I was happy having a glass of wine on the couch enjoying the glow from my Christmas tree with my sweet little man sleeping in bed, while someone was waiting to hurt me. The thought was horrifying.

DURING THIS TIME, I was given a heads up that the defense knew about my journal, what is now this book. I was told they might request a court order to get a copy of it. When I questioned what I could do, the investigators said an option was to hire a personal lawyer to fight it, if it came down to it. *(Because I could afford that, hah!).*

Life kept getting more challenging and stressful. The wrinkles were forming on my face before my eyes. The silver strands of wisdom in my hair were glowing and thriving. But I kept on the forefront of my mind: I can do this; I am a warrior; I am a lioness, and a lioness always protects her cub.

THE WEEK of August 16 I received an email from Claire that Ms. Galewski wanted to meet with me to discuss offering a plea deal. My first initial thought was, *Oh hell no.*

I met with Ms. Galewski right before the final Default Omnibus Hearing. Here were some of the key points and risks of a jury trial vs. a plea deal:

1. He could be found not guilty.
2. The defense could try to throw out the grand jury indictment, which would mean Jesse would be facing only twelve years and serve likely only two-thirds of that.
3. It could be a hung jury and we would have to repeat the trial.

There were multiple risks. The defense would surely try to

make me look like a drug user and an awful person. Did I want to go through that?

Hell yes. For my son. For myself. For the damn cause. For every other rape survivor out there. Abusers do not deserve a "break," nor "a deal."

But what if they do throw out the indictment? Whatever sentence Jesse would be charged with would be our sentence too. Did I want to risk it being only a twelve-year sentence in which he'd only serve eight? Ultimately, it wasn't up to me. The prosecutors represented the entire state, not me as an individual. It was the State of Minnesota vs. Jesse Taylor Anderson.

The offer Ms. Galewski put on the table was a life sentence *with* the possibility of parole. They needed to check with the prison system but believed a life sentence in this situation would be a thirty-year sentence. They would get back to me with more information. After thirty years, he would have the possibility of parole. This would be a deal because the most he would get would be life *without* the possibility of parole.

I emailed Claire a few more questions and gave my final say in the matter (not that it was my decision, but I appreciate that they respected my input). Here is what I said:

[Claire]

I appreciate that the prosecutors asked and respect my opinion regarding the plea deal. Thank you again. As they are aware, I do not believe someone who has committed a crime of such magnitude should be let off easy. Any wrong move on my part would have made this likely a double homicide investigation/trial. I cannot sufficiently describe the amount of fear he instilled in me, particularly now that I know who he is and because I know what he is capable of. I think the offer of life with possibility of parole, with no room for negotiation of anything less is a fine start considering the risks of a Jury Trial.

I hope that upon review of this offer, Jesse and his wife understand the seriousness of the prosecution's side, and that I will not give up (ever) without a strong fight for my son's sake and my own.

Thanks,
Danielle Leukam

I NEEDED to be clear and strong. I had to do and say whatever I could to show that I was not vulnerable anymore. I was not afraid.

24

Support group started up again at the beginning of October. On the evening of October 14 and 15, the Interstate 35W bridge in Minneapolis, Minnesota glowed teal to honor victims and survivors of sexual violence. October 15, 2019 marked two years since the #MeToo movement went viral. To honor those in the Rochester area, I reached out to the Mayor of Rochester and made the request for the City Hall to glow teal as well.

I received an email that maintenance for city hall prefers a thirty days' notice for all light requests. This disheartened me, but I wouldn't give up. After a few emails and phone calls, I finally got the acceptance email that City Hall *would* glow teal!

I was instantly ecstatic. My friends in support group deserved this. Victims and survivors in the Rochester area *deserved* this. And I was honored to facilitate this happening.

Erin drove down on October 14 to hang out and we decided to meet at Buffalo Wild Wings to celebrate. She picked up James from daycare because KTTC, the local news channel, had asked to do an interview with me. I did agree to an interview right after work, as long as it was anonymous.

The lady that interviewed me was incredibly nice. I could hardly believe they wanted to hear from *me*... Some random anonymous chick from Southeast Minnesota simply wanting to make sure her fellow assault survivors would be recognized... It was incredibly cathartic being interviewed. I felt like I finally had a voice, even though it was a faceless one. They only showed my hands on camera, per my request. The clip that was shown on KTTC was short. I felt like I had a *lot* more to say, but I knew my time would come eventually.

When I met James and Erin, they showed up with a little pink bouquet of flowers for me. James said, "I'm so proud of you, Mama!" and my heart that beats for this little man melted.

"Thank you, James! Thank you, Auntie Erin," I said knowing my sister facilitated that lovely surprise. Erin and I ordered dinner and pulled up KTTC on our phones to stream the interview.

"That's so awesome," she said afterwards.

"It felt so good to be able to talk."

After dinner we drove to City Hall to see the lights. That moment was one of the most beautiful things I had ever seen. It felt like step one in my journey to becoming an advocate.

I FORWARDED the media release to the host of support group so she could share it with the other members of the group. Being silent through all of this felt like having an aggressive cancer and going through exhausting, rigorous treatments without being able to tell anyone. I wanted to climb to the top of the tallest building in Rochester and scream what happened to me, but I couldn't. I didn't want anything to be able to be used against me in court. If I said or did the wrong thing, not even knowing what the wrong thing would be, the defense investigator would surely find it to use against me. Or perhaps not, considering I have a clean record other than one *accidental* speeding ticket. I was willing to be an open book for this case. I had nothing to hide. But it was suggested to me by everyone to stay low-key until things were finalized.

Having the support of the mayor and City Hall was my "silent" way of showing local survivors that I would stand with them. They were not alone. They were strong, brave, important, special, and worthy. And they needed to be recognized for the hell they suffered through and are still going through.

It seemed like forever in between each court hearing. The time between kept getting longer and longer. It was nearing the one-year mark since the assault and the next hearing was scheduled for November 4 of 2019.

Prosecutors were going to make a plea deal offer prior to the next hearing. We had a good feeling there would be a slim-to-none chance that Jesse would accept a plea deal anyway. I assumed since he was set on the idea that he would only get two years in prison, agreeing to go to prison for life with possibility of parole would not even be an option for him... especially considering his sixth baby had just been born.

I met with my psychologist whom I had seen last Spring. I felt guilty having to take time off work to go to appointments, but I knew that not only was it helping me personally, but it would also help me be a better mom for James. I updated her on everything with the case and the minimal progress that had been made with my mom and me. After updating her on everything, she said my life was like a country song. And it was. A bad one.

We did a type of therapy called Eye Movement Desensitization and Reprocessing (EMDR). The image that was in my mind nearly every night was Jesse standing at the end of my bed holding a gun pointed at my face. With this therapy, it less-ened the intensity of the image. It made the image black and white, and then it faded. At one point I burst out crying, completely out of nowhere. The therapy was exhausting, that's for sure, but with each session the image got less vivid and less intense. I was surprised by this because it wasn't a tangible therapy; I didn't think it would work. But it did.

In the end, she told me I was a strong woman and to keep doing what I was doing. She told me she was proud of me, and I truly needed to hear that.

The next court hearing was less than three weeks away. One step closer to closure.

Just hang in there, I told myself.

25

It had been a struggle maintaining independence during my healing journey. My stubbornness kept insisting, *I don't need anyone*. But, in fact, I *did* need support. Honestly, I even had a guy who was courting me ask, "Why don't you need me?"

I glanced at him and without a second thought replied, "I don't need anyone."

That wasn't entirely true, of course. But I didn't want to depend on *anyone*. I would *not* let myself look vulnerable, so instead, I acted tough as nails.

Cody and I hung out a lot over the summer of 2019. It was nice having him home from working on the road and it was a change for me to have consistent help with James. We tried to mend things but after a couple of months we decided things weren't much different from before we got divorced. So there we were again, parting ways.

We had planned to go to a Minnesota Wild hockey game at the Excel Center with James with tickets we had gotten from Cody's mom over the summer. It was only a couple of weeks after we decided not to be together anymore. While we were at the game, we were having a great time. We were best friends, co-parenting, enjoying our time "apart" but together as friends. During the start of the game, Cody was leaning forward texting on his phone when he received a photo from a girl.

Huh.

"Oh, who is that?" I asked innocently since it was so blatantly obvious that I could see his phone right in front of me.

"A girl that I'm talking to now," he replied.

Heart. Shattered. On the floor. In a bloody mess. Someone call a janitor. And 911.

I had no words. Only hurt. I ran up the steps and sobbed. I cried my eyes out as moms and dads together held their child's hand walking through the chaos of the Excel Center. I sobbed as I picked up my phone and called my sister, "I want to go home!" I sobbed for a long time until I was well enough to regain my composure, talk it through with my sister, and calm down enough to go back and sit by James and Cody to finish watching the game.

Truly, Cody did nothing wrong. We were divorced. He was allowed to talk to and see other people. But that didn't mean it wasn't painful. He was my best friend and I still loved him; I had wished so badly it had worked for us, but I couldn't hold onto him if we didn't make each other happy.

I silently cried during the game, trying to hide the hurt from my son. I made sure after the game Cody knew he didn't do anything wrong; I was just hurt. It wasn't him; it was *me.*

What the hell was wrong with me? *Well, Danielle, you're obviously not over him.*

Why, since I was obviously capable of being independent, was I still in love with him? For a lot of reasons I'm sure, but because he was safe, he was comfort, and he was someone I trusted who was already in my bubble. I had put up a brick wall after Jesse came along but Cody was already behind the wall with me.

THE STIGMA of being a survivor is that you must be silent. First, I was silent as ordered by Jesse. Second, I was silent as recommended by the investigators. Third, I was silent as suggested by my family. Fourth, I was silent because who wants to hear stories of trauma and hurt and rape anyway? It was the stigma associated with being a survivor: stay silent and carry on with your life. Get over it.

Nope.

Being silent was not part of my healing path. I did it when I had to, but when given the opportunity, like in support group, I talked. That was what helped me heal along with hearing validation, support, opinions, and empathy. Being silent and internalizing anxiety and stress had given me hives, panic attacks and a short temper. It was why I drank far more than I ever used to.

Everything that I was doing was to specifically try to avoid letting myself appear to be vulnerable. I upgraded my Dodge Charger to a Ford F-150 because when I needed to move big things, I wanted to be able to do it myself without having to borrow someone's truck. Also, I felt bigger, badder, and tougher in a truck. Men don't rape tough women, right?

When I told Cody about my struggle with staying silent, he said, "The investigators want you to keep quiet during the case so nothing gets out, then they always have the upper hand. You will have your time to talk soon. Be patient. His life will be over, and yours will begin again."

Yes. This was why I loved him.

. . .

I WAS HAVING a lot of stress and anxiety from work on top of thinking about the upcoming court hearing. I had emailed Claire to ask if they were closing in on making the plea deal offer (still, not fully supportive, but understanding he likely wouldn't accept it anyway) because my anxiety was nearly through the roof.

Sure enough, the stress-filled day was followed by a nightmare. In that nightmare was Jesse. I don't remember anyone else specifically, but it was in a courtroom, presumably at the next court hearing. He was close enough to me that he picked up pencils that were on the desk in front of him and did a backhanded swing at me trying to stab me. I later remembered that he had accepted the plea deal offer and stared at me like, "Now you're fucked," indicating he had some plan to break out of prison or something.

I woke up terrified.

There was a lump in my throat all morning and I felt nauseous. I was extra cautious on the way to work. My boss and a friend brought me a breakfast sandwich and a cup of coffee, despite having already eaten breakfast at home. I needed the comfort and warmth in my stomach. My dear friends made the day bearable, and of course the distraction of my job helped too.

I didn't tell my family about the dream. I was sure they would tell me to go talk to my therapist anyway. My therapist was amazing, but I still felt guilty having to leave work, so I didn't see her as much as I probably should have. I wasn't putting myself first; I was just trying to stuff my feelings down to try to make my life as normal as possible, which meant *not* seeing a therapist. I felt like I was in a decent place mentally a lot of the time, besides, my therapist wouldn't have brought me a breakfast sandwich on a warm, delicious English muffin. And that was what I needed.

·   ·   ·

SOMETIMES ON TIMEHOP, the app on my phone that gathers my photos from years past on that same day, I would see photos of myself from years and years ago. It was awesome reminiscing. But in November of 2019 I came across photos that I took in November 2018... James and I at the gym, his Halloween costume, fun times with my girlfriends... and I felt like I was in the Twilight Zone. When I saw the photos I thought, *Oh, this was when I was happy. This was when my life was in order. This was when I was healthy and did Sober-October and went to the gym four days a week. Here was the screenshot of my 7.12 mile jog on a frosty morning in late October. Here was the Halloween Party at Bowlocity.* I was seeing these photos remembering how happy I was but knowing there was impending doom. I saw myself enjoying the crisp air, my friends, the gym, and my mom back in 2018.

What I also thought about when I scrolled through Timehop was that Jesse had access to these pictures. We knew he took pictures from my phone so when I scrolled through, I thought, *Was it this one? The one of me in my sports bra so I could compare the progress of months at the gym? The videos of me critiquing myself doing box jumps? This photo that was meant for my eyes only?* I kept thinking about all of the possibilities he could have done with these photos. Look at them for his own pleasure, sell them online, make hurtful Memes out of them. I didn't know, but I would get disgusted, nauseous, and angry thinking about it.

THE WEEK prior to the court hearing in November, I received an email from Claire. It said they had received a message from the public defender's office indicating they have been alerted to a conflict of interest with the case and the case would need to be reassigned to different public defenders.

Claire didn't have many details to share with me other than the defense was asking that the hearing be postponed so the case could be reassigned to a different public defender. Claire's email went on to say, *Given these changes, the prosecutors will not be making a plea offer at this time.*

The next two emails didn't have much additional information with exception that Judge Leahy, who was assigned to the case, granted the continuance and that the hearing would be rescheduled for within the next two months.

As anyone can guess, this had my mind going. I pondered every situation I could think of. I hated not knowing everything that was happening, and I was sure it was because of some manipulative plan Jesse had done or had in mind.

OVER THE WEEKEND I went to a birthday party at my old neighbor's house for their son. James was best friends with to the two neighbor kids and it was heartbreaking when we had to move away. I knew James was going to be excited to see the neighbors, so I didn't hesitate for a second to RSVP "Yes!"

I buckled James up in his booster seat in my truck, called Cody, and we headed over to our old neighbors' house. On our way through St. Charles, I passed the old familiar Subway on Highway 14, the Kwik Trip on the right across from Good Sport Bar and Grill on the left, and the Fire Station after that. We cruised up the road, past the high school, over the hill to see the John Deere on the left before turning left towards my old neighborhood. We took the first right into the neighborhood, and another, then I made a U-turn at the end of the road to park in front of my old house.

I shifted the truck into park just before James jumped out to greet Cody in his car in front of us. I nonchalantly looked over at my old house and saw the bird bath Cody had bought me years ago tipped over into the snow like a piece of junk. I instantly burst into flaming hot tears. No warning, no preparation, no build up, no one by my side. Out of nowhere, my face was filled with large, uncontrollable tears as I was parked in front of my perfect, split level home with the bird bath I had accidentally left in the front lawn laying worthlessly in the snow.

James and Cody were walking to the neighbors' house where the party was when James noticed me still in the truck and saw I was crying, struggling to breathe. He came running back to the truck, opened the passenger door, crawled up inside yelling, "Mommy! Mommy! What's wrong!"

"Oh, no, honey. It's okay. Mommy's okay." Mom-mode kicked in and I pretended to have myself put back together as much as I could.

Cody noticed and came back to my truck as well, "You okay?" He stood at my door as James continued to question what was going on.

"Mommy, you're crying."

I held it together for James's sake enough to reply, "I just noticed Mommy left the bird bath at the old house! I can't believe I did that. I'm just sad." After that, I dried my face, put my shoulders back, got out of the truck and went to the party.

Just like that, PTSD had appeared out of nowhere like a ton of bricks and I had to pretend everything was perfectly fine, despite the sharp, broken pieces inside my heart. Maybe having to quickly suppress my tears in front of my son contributed to me feeling like I had a black soul. I wore black, bought black things and associated this with my black soul. People would giggle at this and would tell me I was a ray of sunshine, but I certainly didn't feel that way.

Much like Roxane Gay in her incredible memoir entitled, *Hunger*, I wanted my body to portray an image that would keep me safe. While Roxane Gay ate and ate and ate creating a larger body that she felt safe in, I've altered my body to appear as though I do not want to be, nor should I be fucked with. I no longer wanted to be the girl next door—the girl in the flower sundress. I wanted to be a badass. I wanted to be intimidating. I turned dark.

I WAS glad to have the support group to bring up these dark feelings. One of the hosts showed us how to look up criminal records and I asked that they check Jesse Taylor Anderson as an example. Jesse's record housed a whole list of previous charges including speeding tickets, but there was also a charge that showed cruelty to animals, a dog. I had known this vaguely already, but it hit hard when it was discussed at group, proving even more what kind of person he was.

There was a girl in group who was feeling broken. To spare the details for confidentiality purposes, she was explaining how she felt broken and shattered into a million pieces. What came to mind for me was my necklace I had bought for myself from Bryan Anthonys, a jewelry company. I was wearing the necklace called "Beautifully Broken," so I pulled out the message that came with it and asked if I could read it to her. With consent, I read:

*"Let go of the idea of perfection – you are not perfect, you are real.
Let yourself be flawed, and allow yourself to make mistakes.
Recognize that you're not always going to have it all together.
Sometimes your heart is going to break, you are going to get hurt,
you are going to feel pain. Don't apologize for being broken – every
time you break you become a little more alive. You become more
open with yourself. You become exposed to your sensibility. Every
crack tells you a little more about yourself – your strength, your*

courage, your tenacity – what you're made of. Do not hide these pieces from the world, they are a part of who you are. You see, the most beautiful people are beautifully broken. Their hearts are heavy but they love the deepest, they have seen the dark but they appreciate everything that shines. They're compassionate, understanding, and empathetic. Beautiful hearts just don't happen – and you my dear are going to show the world just how beautiful you are."

I GAVE her my necklace from around my neck and told her, "This is so you never feel alone. We," I gestured to everyone in the group, "are here with you and here for you. You are strong, and you are beautiful. You're never alone."

Giving her that necklace was incredibly rewarding. I had grown to learn that healed people heal people. And healing people was healing. This was yet another reason why networking with other survivors was an incredible feeling. We had the opportunity to help each other rather than just ourselves.

TIME WAS TICKING by and nearing November 17 and 18. One of the only consistent forms of therapy I had was writing. It was too cold to ride my motorcycle so instead I was inside with my journal and beer whenever I wasn't working or taking care of James, the puppy, and the cats, which took up a majority of my time.

I felt like I was waiting for impending rest. Waiting to process and recover. Waiting to have a voice. Because I was kept busy trying to maintain my life and family and job, lengthy recovery wasn't something I had time for. Sometimes I was so busy that avoidance and bottling things up was what I did to get through the day. But regardless of how busy I was, the assault still consumed my mind.

I began experiencing more triggers nearing the one-year mark from the attack. The weather was a trigger. It was the light dusting of snow on my new driveway, the bare trees, the white, snow-covered fields, and cloudy skies that all reminded me of his footprints down my driveway and the drone footage of his path through the field. My visible breath floating from my lips and through the air reminded me of that day. Darkness filling the sky earlier and earlier in the day made me feel uneasy.

THE WEEK PRECEDING the weekend of the seventeenth and eighteenth was awful. I was acutely depressed, there were many triggers, and I truly felt like Robin Williams: putting on a smile when I was dying inside. I felt so broken that I made a point to tell my closest friends I felt like Robin Williams because I was truly scared for myself.

One of the few people that took me seriously in saying this was my boss, Jenny.

"Let's go to lunch. We need to catch up," she said.

"Okay. If you're sure you have time." I didn't want my outside-of-work feelings to be an inconvenience.

When we got to lunch, she gave me her look (the look I would have given her too) as though she was peering into my soul, wanting to know, "What's going on?"

I let myself break down. I was finally feeling like someone genuinely cared and took the time to hear me. I could be honest with her because she and I were so much alike. She understood, she validated, and she listened. She and her heart of gold sincerely understood how terrible I felt.

"I'm afraid," I said. "I'm afraid because of how awful I feel. It hurts so much. I sit in my truck and cry, and it takes me ten minutes to calm down enough to walk into work. It's not because of work, but because I still feel so alone sometimes. I'm just... I'm just afraid." Was feeling that way what people felt like before they hurt themselves?

I DIDN'T HEAR MUCH from my family around this time with the exception of my sister. I went up to the cities on Friday, November 15, to spend time with her and her wife. On the sixteenth I was alone, but on the seventeenth I had decided we should throw a party. The seventeenth was hardest for me because it was the day I was *so* happy while he was waiting to hurt me. It was my last day of innocence.

That day, my sister, Cody and I watched football, ate food, and put together my Christmas tree. One of the girls from support group stopped by as well. I had to make new memories on that date, and I was grateful to not be alone.

James had a sense that something was going on. I don't know what words he might have caught during our conversations, but he brought the party to a dead stop when he asked, "Mommy, do you remember when we met Memaw at the grocery store and you were crying?"

....*I'm sorry, what?* I knew exactly what he was referring to.

"Do you remember, Mommy?"

"Yes, I do, love. I do remember," I replied not knowing what else to say.

James's four-year-old attention span changed the subject shortly thereafter, probably to wanting a snack, but he knew what was going on. He knew why we were all together. Those words he said pierced my soul like I couldn't have imagined. He shouldn't know what happened nor why we were all together. I hated that he remembered... I hated that sometimes it *did* get talked about in front of him. I hated that someday he would figure out what happened and how Jesse hurt his mommy... I was not ready for that day to come. I'll never be ready.

ONE OF THE hosts of support group had emailed me an application for the Survivor Advisory Group to the Governor. It was a joint group from Violence Free Minnesota, Sacred Hoop Coalition, Minnesota Coalition Against Sexual Assault, and Minnesota Indian Women's Sexual Assault Coalition. Obligations were monthly meetings, two to three hours in length in Saint Paul for twelve months, including meetings with the Governor, Lt. Governor and staff, and reviewing materials outside of the meetings.

I did not hesitate to apply; I wanted to participate in anything I could to advocate against sexual violence. I was beyond thrilled to even have the chance to apply to something like this!

A couple of weeks later I got an email that said I was selected to participate as a member of the group. As soon as I read the email while I was at work, I started jumping up and down, and said, "Oh. My. God!" I would have a chance to participate in a group that could make changes for the better.

Later that day I received another email from Claire notifying me that the Contested hearing was rescheduled for January 21, 2020. This pushed us out nine weeks. She went on to say the defense attorney would have a chance to bring forth any legal challenges they saw with the case, and they would likely have officers who worked on the case testify.

I HAD a couple of days of PTO mid-December of 2019 and on my first day off I woke up from a nightmare with congestion, a pounding headache, and coughing that felt like needles trying to crawl their way out of my chest. My sweet German Shepherd, Leona, crawled on top of my chest, laid her head next to mine, and licked my arm.

This cold developed a cough that would last well into January. On my days off, I was finally able to sit down to write. I was sick for much of the week, but that didn't stop me from having a voice, if only in writing.

26

4:30 a.m.

I couldn't afford to get my little man a lot of gifts, so instead I decorated the kitchen with everything I could find for his fifth birthday. I hung streamers on the kitchen light, hung up a "Happy Birthday!" banner, set out superhero napkins and cups, then continued to get ready for work.

When it was time to wake up my little man, I opened his bedroom door and all sixty-five pounds of Leona's eight-month-old German Shepherd body jumped onto James's bed and woke him up with a nose nudge to his cheek and a tongue across his face. She then went over to sniff behind his bed to make sure the coast was clear. She stayed in the room with him until he crawled out of bed.

"Happy fifth birthday!" I said as I snuggled his face next to mine.

Little Man ate breakfast, got dressed, and loaded up his cookies to take to daycare for his birthday treat.

. . .

AFTER A HALF DAY OF WORK, I left to go to Winona to meet with Claire and Ms. Galewski to have a brief meeting prior to the court hearing that was set for the following week.

"The initial charges Jesse was facing would be a twelve-year sentence. We doubled that to get twenty-four years, and that would be the number of years he would serve if he took the 'life in prison with the possibility for parole' plea deal," Ms. Galewski explained.

We were initially thinking life meant a thirty-year sentence, but that would be for murder. For the crimes Jesse committed with the heinous element would be twenty-four years. We then had to figure out if the "Good Time" rule applied. Could he be facing a mere sixteen years? It was a question yet to be answered.

"If I told you I'm not supportive of the plea deal anymore, would you still make the offer?" I questioned.

"Yes," Mrs. Galewski replied. She was excellent at her job and explaining things. She was by the book and despite the situation we were in, I could tell she was a wonderful human.

But I cried. I cried because sixteen years wasn't enough, because twenty-four years wasn't enough. In twenty-four years, my son would only be twenty-nine years old. I cried because when my son leaves my locked-down house to go to college, he'll probably have to have a confidential address as well, right? When Jesse is released from prison, we're all going to need to have a confidential address. And what if my son has a wife and children by this time? Would their lives be in danger too?

We also discussed that the defense may still request more time to review the evidence for the case. That was a clue for me to prepare for the hearing the following week to be continued again. I was a rollercoaster of emotions upon leaving the meeting. I was still sure Jesse wouldn't take the plea deal, but I guess only time would tell, and I would be notified of his decision when he made one.

. . .

THE NEXT DAY was January 15, my mom's birthday. I attended the first Survivor Advisory Group meeting in the cities. The hour-and-a-half drive was a challenge in the snow... but I'm from Minnesota, so just another day, really. I entered the building, found the conference room, introduced myself to those who were there, and sat patiently waiting for the rest of the group.

Happy birthday, Mom! I texted as I was waiting.

As people started rolling in, a slender brunette came in and sat by me.

"Hi. I'm Sarah. It's nice to meet you!" she said.

"Hi. I'm Danielle. Nice to meet you too!"

...wait. Sarah?

"May I ask your last name?" I asked.

"Super," she replied.

I instantly became speechless. I couldn't form words but was attempting to, so all I was doing was blushing and slurring, but I managed to get out, "Oh! Can I shake your hand?"

She politely said yes, and I quickly told her it was an honor to meet her, though it may have come out in toddler articulation. Sarah Super was a public figure who I have idolized since the day I listened to an episode of a podcast in which she told her survival story. And here she was, sitting right next to me.

The two-hour meeting ensued, and I was in awe every second of it. I was surrounded by a group of incredibly special, diverse survivors as well as the directors of coalitions that facilitated the group. It was an honor to be there.

THE FOLLOWING Tuesday was January 21, the Contested Omnibus Hearing. I still hadn't had a consistent Victim's Advocate from Winona County to attend with me (I seemed to get a new one every few months), but I had Cody by my side and Claire from the courthouse.

When the judge entered, the hearing started rolling. The defense requested bail to be lowered to a manageable amount so Jesse could be on house arrest. The prosecution listed all the charges that are pending against Jesse to elaborate on why it was not safe for him to be out of jail.

"Your honor, additionally, Mr. Anderson has sexual misconduct charges against a vulnerable adult in Kandiyohi County, as well as charges in Hennepin County and firearm charges in Kandiyohi County," the prosecutor said, reiterating her point.

Hearing of the firearms charges was new to me. Supposedly he had guns in his possession that were not his. He allegedly stole them from a job site because he was not happy with the amount of money he was paid for the job. Upon hearing the pending charges, the judge quickly replied, "Request denied. Mr. Anderson is a flight risk due to the additional charges he was indicted with. Bail will stay at $2 million."

The defense and prosecution then started talking about the grand jury transcript and a secret conversation Jesse was trying to have over the phone with a privately hired attorney from Kandiyohi County. The fact that he had a privately hired attorney blew my mind. The grand jury transcript had been given back to the Winona Offices, but no one had gone through to make sure all the pages were accounted for. What the conversation over the phone sounded like was that he sent his private attorney things to give to his ex-wife. They had gotten divorced the previous summer, but Jesse and his ex-wife seemed to still be together. Because of attorney/client privilege, correction officers are not able to look through that type of mail. Meaning, he could have written his ex-wife a message on these documents or any piece of paper that was never caught.

The judge ordered the grand jury transcript to be gone through page-by-page to be sure that none of the pages were missing. I felt like I was saying, "What?! How does he keep doing sketchy, manipulative crap even behind bars?"

As expected, the defense did request more time to go through the evidence and the Contested Omnibus Hearing was ultimately rescheduled for April 15. Three months out.

I FOUND out the next week that all pages of the grand jury transcript *were* accounted for. But that still didn't mean Jesse didn't do something shady with his new attorney even without those pages. Why else would he be having a secret conversation? Was the attorney a family friend who could have been doing him a favor? There were so many possibilities. So many theories running through my mind.

IN MARCH OF 2020, Minnesota started shutting down. COVID-19 had made its way from overseas to the United States, finding its way to Minnesota and to Olmsted County where I resided. Work became chaotic, and I was trying to calm the storm as the charge nurse. Bars and restaurants in Minnesota shut down from March 17 to May 5. The economy was crashing, and record numbers of people were filing for unemployment.

Cody and I tried to live together again, ultimately ending in a third separation mid-March when everything started shutting down due to COVID-19, and when the United States of America was starting to go into panic mode. I had just joined a kick-boxing gym in Rochester called Ferrell's eXtreme Bodyshaping with an amazing owner and crew of people, but after a few weeks could no longer attend because I stopped having consistent help with James and because of the COVID-19 shutdowns.

Unsurprisingly, I was notified in the beginning of April that the Contested Omnibus Hearing would be postponed *yet again* due to COVID-19 and because the defense had not filed anything for the hearing yet. *Shocking.*

One measly piece of good news during the pandemic was that I finally got my bird bath from my old house. I also got my two solar powered lights from the front yard that the new owners of my old house were willing to give to Cody. I put my bird bath in my new landscaping and filled it up with water. It was a simple ornament that provided me with a small feeling of "home."

27

THE GOOSEBUMPS STUNG MY LEGS AS I WALKED DOWN THE HALL towards work. It was 7:20 am, six and a half hours until the hearing. I wasn't cold. I guessed the goosebumps reflected my nerves. Rebreathing my own breath under my mask (required because of COVID-19) was not refreshing, and I needed to be refreshed. But I didn't think fresh air was going to cut it.

I could go for a hug... to be wrapped up in someone's arms, feeling warm and loved; somewhere that feels like home. And rest my head on someone's chest where I would be safe and could forget about the world for just a moment. But whose? Whose hug, whose arms, whose chest? I was reminded that while I had support, it was only myself I could rely on one-hundred percent of the time. I couldn't put that dependence on anyone. Despite feeling lonely, I had become even better at pushing people away and keeping them at a distance.

I caught myself staring at the floor as I walked through the skyway. I was following the lines on the floor, watching my shoes carry me mindlessly forward. I knew the path, and I knew I wasn't going to run into anything. My head was down with droopy eyes and a somber face, trying to be invisible.

Somehow I realized what I was doing; I forced my chin up and thought, *Face the world head on. You got this.*

And I did. I didn't have to convince myself, just remind myself. I needed to make it through the morning at work, a perfect distraction, then I would be going home to log onto my computer and watch the court hearing from my house via Zoom.

I ANXIOUSLY WAITED AT HOME, counting the minutes leading up to the hearing. I was manically cleaning until the hearing started. I first noticed there were already multiple people logged on. My profile picture and name were the second thing I noticed, and I immediately changed my picture and my name to "Victim." Shortly thereafter, *he* popped on... his orange jumpsuit stood out. His face mask gave me chills down my spine. When the judge said, "Give the camera a wave if you can hear me," he lifted his hands and gave the camera an awkward wave. I could tell the handcuffs may have been attached to either a table or his ankles. His resemblance to Hannibal Lecter gave me nausea and anxiety I naturally suppressed in front of my ex-husband, who was watching with me. I wanted to appear to be calm, cool, collected, and strong. I was afraid he wouldn't console me, and I didn't want to experience that feeling.

The two-hour hearing proceeded then ended on a note that there would have to be a Part Two to finish the remaining testimonies including possibly one from Jesse.

THE NEXT DAY MY NEIGHBOR, a kind Vietnamese man, saw right through me. I was outside doing yard work and he came over to look at my fence to see how he could help me fix it.

"If you have no one to help you, I will help you," he said.

"Thank you! That's so nice. I mean, I should be okay. I don't want to inconvenience you," I replied.

He took a moment before saying, "You don't have anyone to help you. I will help you." Could people really be this kind without having a motive?

"You ride a motorcycle and drive a big truck. You appear to be strong. But you need to be strong on the inside," as he taps his fingers on his temple and gazes into my eyes. "You control your mind," he goes on to say. "You need to be strong on the inside. You ride your motorcycle, and it helps you forget. It makes you feel strong and helps you forget the past *while* you are riding. But what about when you get home? You're all alone. You can control your mind and your energy, and what you put your energy into."

I didn't know what to say. I was dumbfounded that someone could clearly see my feelings and put them into words that accurately described what was happening.

"Yeah..." What else could I say?

I guess I thought I was doing a great job at hiding the truth, but clearly not from everyone. And that was okay. I'd wear my heart on my sleeve... maybe quite literally, considering the new lioness tattoo I'd just gotten.

I've got this, I told myself. *Just as a lioness would.*

THE CONTESTED OMNIBUS Hearing ended up happening in three parts, because two wasn't enough to cover everything. Reading had become an obsession for me. I hardly ever watched Netflix and Hulu anymore, but rather got lost in books. I loved learning with Malcolm Gladwell but also getting lost in novels, losing myself in other peoples' stories so I could escape my own.

I also spent a *lot* of time riding my motorcycle with Jake. Every time James was with his dad, Jake and I would hop on the bikes for a wind-therapy session. We'd stick a couple of Coors Light pints into the saddle bags with a baggie of jalapeño-stuffed green olives and ride out to Elba where we'd park the bikes and have a beer on the side of a low-mainte-nance road we called, "The Marsh" (like from *Where the Craw-dads Sing,* by Delia Owens). It was glorious. And when the weather was too bad for bikes, we'd have our two-beer-Tues-days at Newts, the home of the best cheeseburgers in Rochester.

IN JULY, I lost ten pounds in one week. A series of painful events happened. Sure enough, my "bad things happen in threes" streak was in full force. I was being protective of my sister, worried because she wasn't talking to me very much anymore. I was concerned. In her eyes, I went too far, and it caused me to lose the rock-solid relationship I had with her. We didn't talk for months.

Heartbroken and hopeless, I confided in my best friend Jake. I told him my relationship with my sister abruptly ended, leaving out private details, but he didn't think I did enough. It was the opposite of what my sister wanted, but it didn't matter. I couldn't get it right for either of them. Because we had such a big disagreement, he stopped talking to me, and I let him. My best friend, my ride or die, my number one fan was my second loss.

And on the third day, I found out Cody had a girlfriend. He told me he didn't care about my personal life anymore. This pushed me over the edge, causing me to drown in heartbreak and loneliness. My mind could not handle losing the three most important people in my life and I became physically ill.

I spent a lot of time by myself in the summer of 2020. I felt alone. I *was* alone. I didn't have to be, but the physical ailments caused me to push everyone away. I even tried to push away

Anne, my other best friend, but she cared too much to let me. I didn't want to reach out to family or friends like Anna and Katie (some of the people I had been confiding in) because, as friends do, they would ask, "How's it going?" and I knew I'd lose my composure. Instead, I consumed my time with running and it became an awesome form of therapy for me, next to the wind therapy riding motorcycle provided.

I sold the Harley Street 750 I had for a Harley Dyna, and it was *far* more comfortable. It made me feel in control, something I had been significantly lacking yet needing. It was just me, the bike, and the open road. I basically had to be pried off the bike, something only the darkness and *occasionally* the weather could do.

On top of being in control of my motorcycle, I knew I was losing weight in an unhealthy manner, but the idea of losing even more weight by running became an obsession. It was another thing I could control—what I ate, how much I ran, and ultimately my weight.

I lost control when a gun was pointed at my head, when I was zip tied, when I was raped repeatedly, and when my son's life was threatened. I lost control when I couldn't help my sister and when I didn't do what my best friend Jake wanted me to do. I lost control when my ex-husband, who I still loved and wanted to be with even though we didn't make each other as happy as we used to, found a girlfriend.

Buying things I couldn't afford, such as my truck, made me feel in control (though reckless). Are you seeing the pattern?

I *didn't* have a good head on my shoulders after this; I was a wreck. I was at the bottom of a quicksand pit, stuck, with only myself to rely on to crawl my way out of what seemed like an impossible situation. I had stress-induced anorexia, and no one could see I was dying inside because I was a master at hiding it. I gagged from taking a vitamin because I simply couldn't put anything into my body. My fingers grew cold, my lips grew tingly; I was starving. As much as I didn't *want* to feel the way I felt about my ex-husband because he had a girlfriend and as much as I *wanted* to be close with my sister and mend my relationship with Jake, the feelings were like a cancer, uncontrollably destroying me one day at a time. They were bold and heavy, drowning me in darkness.

"Are you eating?" Anne asked me one day at work.

"...Not really. I get sick when I eat," I admitted.

"Have you told anyone? Have you talked to your therapist about it?"

"No. It's not a big deal. I mean, I'm eating some. I'm fine," I replied. My famous words, *I'm fine.*

"I'm worried about you... what can I do?" Anne asked.

"I was thinking about making an appointment with my therapist... I'll do that on my lunch break," I bargained.

"Promise you'll tell her what's going on?" she asked, concerned.

"I promise," I said, and I meant it. Again, I was afraid for myself and how I was feeling. The go-to people I would have talked to about this would have been my sister, Jake, or Cody. And Jenny too, of course, but I didn't like bringing my home life to work, yet another thing I was a master at doing. Talking about it meant thinking about it, and I didn't want to do that either. I couldn't tell my sister how heartbroken I was that Cody had found someone else. I couldn't tell Jake how much I missed my sister. And then, to top it off, I stopped having Cody's support at court hearings and everything in between.

BACK AT WORK I felt like I was living a double life. What my co-workers saw: normal, stable, single, working mom. What I felt: broken, PTSD, triggers, empty, depression, anxiety... survivor, but ready to be the world's biggest advocate.

My guard dog Leona and I were spending a Sunday

morning together without James. I was manically cleaning again—a task I'd zone-out doing to relieve stress. I was scrubbing my entire kitchen; it was productive escapism. The side of the stove needed detailing, so I was on the floor scrubbing when I abruptly paused. *What the hell am I doing?* I noticed the rain trickling down my patio door. I stopped and listened; an air came over me and I found peace in the rain. I followed the peace, the calm, the serenity. Leona and I went to the garage where I opened the car-door and grabbed a lawn chair. There I sat with my ankles crossed leaning back as she lay at my feet, enjoying the white noise that drowned the chaos within my brain.

And I was okay.

JAKE and I mended our disagreement in late August. He knew that regardless of what he wanted me to do, I was going to do my own thing and he needed to respect that. "You stubborn Tilford girls!" he would say referring to my sister and me.

We went on a motorcycle ride on Labor Day. It was a high of 58 degrees and scattered storms in the area. But it was a day off work I needed to take advantage of on the bike, so I put on my long johns, jeans, boots, sweater, coat, gloves, Neckie, helmet, and off we went. We made it to Wisconsin before it started raining. We stopped for a Bloody Mary and tried to track the storm on our phones. It was getting worse as time passed, and we had no way out, so we decided to go straight through the storm back to Rochester.

The rain was coming down as we got onto our bikes. As we took off towards Rochester going through Wabasha, I passed Jake on my motorcycle with my fist in the air, laughing out loud and yelled, "David Goggins!" and sped away (going the speed limit, of course).

David Goggins is the author of *Can't Hurt Me,* an inspirational book about how he had a rough childhood but mastered his own mind and grew up to be unstoppable. A David Goggins video I recently watched called *The Cure to Laziness*, stated: *"Because tomorrow I get to do the same fucking shit again, man. Whatever the shit is that made me fucking nauseous and sick to my stomach, that made me hurt, there's no ending! And that's the person I listen to. That's the person who's gained knowledge, who gained knowledge through suffering! And on the other end of the suffering is a world very few, very few have ever seen. It's a beautiful world! That's where you find yourself.*

On the other end of suffering is a beautiful world—that's where you find yourself. I appreciated life far more than I did prior to that morning. What I needed to do now was appreciate myself again as an individual. I needed to recognize the strength and determination I carried to push forward. And it's true. The world was so beautiful on the other side, once I accomplished the seemingly impossible task of loving myself.

IN LATE SUMMER OF 2020, Jesse had caught an error on the search warrant from when the investigators searched his truck. He found that the truck listed on the warrant was his 2005 white Ford truck rather than his 2016 white Ford truck.

Jesse had a 2005 truck that was crashed and totaled in the past. Because it wasn't sold, it was still listed on the DMV website as being in his possession. His 2016 truck was bought by his wife, so it was listed under *her* name. When the investigators searched the DMV website, they had only searched for vehicles Jesse owned; they did not search his wife's name.

Because of the error on the search warrant, the defense requested to reopen the Contested Omnibus Hearing. The judge granted the request and there was a hearing on October 7 of 2020.

Prior to the hearing, Mrs. Galewski wanted to meet with me

(which I knew was never a good sign). She wanted to give me a heads up that the court hearing probably wasn't going to go in our favor. Even though Jesse's wife had given verbal consent for the search of *her* truck, that wouldn't have been good enough. After the defense and prosecution both resubmitted their briefings, it was likely that the judge would throw out the evidence found in the truck because the warrant was inaccurate. Additionally, the video Jesse had on his phone, other evidence from his phone, DNA evidence, and his initial statement the morning following his arrest were all in question because of minor details, wording, and technicalities. It was normal for the defense attorneys to try to question anything and everything they could, but for me as the victim it didn't feel right; it didn't feel like justice.

A comment Ms. Galewski made to the judge during the hearing went something like this, "And isn't it true that [your ex-wife] bought the vehicle for you because you were having financial troubles due to a drug problem?"

The answer was, "Yes."

That, at least, made me laugh.

I RECEIVED an email from Claire on November 3 stating the prosecution wanted to meet with me because of a deal the defense had brought up. I instantly had a ton of emotions I could not control nor pinpoint.

Anger? Anger because if the defense was bringing up a plea deal, it was likely something Jesse was on board with, which meant it sure as hell wouldn't be good enough.

Relief? Relief that an end may be in sight sooner than I had thought?

Stress and defeat? Because I knew the decision wasn't ultimately up to me. I felt like there was nothing I could do anyway.

. . .

I MET with Ms. Galewski the following morning in Winona. "The plea deal will sentence him to 250 months in prison. When you do the math, it is just under twenty-one years," Ms. Galewski told me.

"But he'll only have to serve two-thirds of that with good time?" I asked referring to the sentencing guidelines in Minnesota that reduces an inmate's term by one day per every two days of good behavior.

"Yes. So that would be just under fourteen years of prison time."

"And he's already served almost two of those years?" I pressed.

"Yes. So it will be about twelve years," she explained.

"And this is a done deal already?"

"Yes. But we still want to know how you feel about it."

I hesitated. I had no idea. My insides felt like a tornado. My mind felt foggy and in shock. It wasn't good enough. Twelve years of prison, when our initial offer was a life sentence with the *possibility* of parole. I trusted Ms. Galewski was doing the right thing. She and Claire had known from the very beginning how I felt about everything, and they didn't want to present a plea deal to me if Jesse wasn't going to take it. I tried to put into words the thoughts running through my mind and the one thing that was evident was, "So my son and I have a sentence of twelve years of freedom."

28

I RECENTLY READ AN INTRIGUING BOOK CALLED *UNTIL WE RECKON* written by Danielle Sered. When I got to this quote, "Hurt people hurt people," I felt like I had an epiphany. I felt like things *clicked* and these simple words *explained* so much in my situation, but also raised many questions.

Another sentence I came across in the next chapter says, "Research unequivocally shows that one of the most sure-fire predictors of violence is surviving it." This solidified my question, *What did Jesse survive to cause him to hurt other people?*

I've been feeling a lot of anger and rage since November of 2018 and I can maintain a calm demeanor a vast majority of the time, but occasionally I snap. And I've admitted to a couple of friends when I find myself seeing red and raging that I'm not afraid to go to jail if someone pokes the bear.

When I say this, I can't express how serious I am. I can't find the right words. My face, my voice... nothing accurately portrays what I feel. I can tell someone, "I'm so mad I'm shaking," or "I'm raging; all I am seeing is red," and sometimes the reply I still get is, "You're still a ray of sunshine."

No, no...You don't understand. Please, listen.

But... bad guys are the ones who hurt people. I shouldn't be feeling like this. But now that I've survived violence, what if *I* become a bad guy?

Truthfully, Jake and my sister had a conversation about this. My sister said, "I'm afraid she's going to stab somebody in the eye with a fork." And then Jake tells me, "No forks for you!" Ha! He was joking, but I felt like this was *truth*. And it was scary. It is scary. I scare myself. I don't want to end up a bad guy. I don't want to be violent. I don't want to see red and rage anymore.

I spoke about my feelings at support group. I said, "I'm not afraid to go to jail if someone pushes me too far or threatens to hurt my son again," and went on to explain how *I feel* the rage that criminals probably feel when they hurt people. It's an awful feeling to acknowledge having; it is a burden to carry that weight.

But one of the hosts told me, "You are on a whole other level of empathy. You are discovering who you are, and you're going to research this, because I know you, and get to an entirely new level of advocating. You may even work *with* perpetrators someday." She enlightened me to the fact that I have empathy and it *can* be used for good. Prior to this, it was just a mind-blowing heavy burden I was feeling.

Knowledge is power. Knowledge is healing. Enlightenment is healing. Understanding is healing. I'm glad to learn more about myself and the effects trauma has caused. Being single can be dangerous. It is dangerous to walk in my shoes. It's not that non-single women don't get raped, but in my case, almost all of the sexual assault and harassment situations I've endured came *after* the perpetrators knew I was separated. It's like they respected Cody and that I was his at the time, more than they respected me solo.

.   .   .

IN HIS BOOK *David and Goliath: Underdogs, Misfits, and the Art of Battling Giants*, Malcolm Gladwell outlines parts of the London Blitz—the German bombing-invasion of London in 1940 and 1941 during World War II—and explains (referencing psychiatrist J.T. MacCurdy) three responses that Londoners had to the Blitz:

1. People who were killed
2. Near misses
3. Remote misses

A NEAR MISS is a narrowly avoided collision or other accident. This results in trauma. These were the Londoners who were impacted by the bombs (likely injured, but survived) and were traumatized by the experience. It resulted in leaving the victims devastated.

A **remote miss** was when the Londoners (in Gladwell's example) heard the attacks and bombings, may have been close to the destruction, but were energized rather than traumatized. In one example, he explains that a family elected to *not* flee London but to stay, excitedly saying something to the extent of... *What? Leave? And miss all of this?!* referring to the nearby bombings. Gladwell says, "A remote miss makes you think you are invincible." It can leave you stronger. Another word associated with a remote miss is invulnerability—the property of being incapable of being hurt, physically or emotionally. It is acquired courage.

Upon reading all this, I reflected on the feelings I had outside of depression and anxiety. The depression started to lift, though the anxiety stayed, and I had new feelings of empowerment. I wondered, *Can being a survivor of being held hostage and raped at gunpoint leave a person feeling like they experienced a remote miss? Can it leave a person feeling invincible? Can it change a person into being a thrill-seeker? Reckless? Energized? Full of new life? Thriving?*

Of course, *I was not missed.* The bomb exploded on me, my life, my house, and my family. But I did not die, that is what the "miss" was, I guess. I fall in the near miss category because yes, I was injured, impacted, traumatized, and devastated. But I also fall in the remote miss category because I started to feel energized, invulnerable, and stronger, like a lioness. Most of all, having acquired courage.

Experiencing the near miss of being traumatized but surviving and living to tell the tale, absolutely sucked. But these feelings that were coming more often now were giving me energy to advocate, write, and be on the path to making some changes for the better for survivors and secondary victims.

I knew I would not become a criminal nor a bad guy because I acknowledged these feelings and took action to heal myself. I was also educated and aware, and instead, using that rage for good. I had become a person who did what I want. No one could tell me what to do. Jake could give advice to not do something then knowingly add, "But I know you're going to do it anyway." I was striving for goals I never thought I would have strived for. I stood for what I thought was right, and I protected my friends and family. I was a ruthless lioness, and of course, I now had ferocious acquired courage. Surviving the lighter side of four pounds of pressure opened my eyes to **living** life, rather than being content.

I NEVER COULD HAVE IMAGINED that trauma could have such an effect on me. I had finally grown to love myself.

29

JESSE PLED GUILTY ON NOVEMBER 20, 2020. THIS COURT HEARING was via Zoom, so I watched it in my home with Cody, Jake, and my mom. Erin couldn't come down because her wife had COVID-19 and she had been directly exposed to her, so she watched at home. The hearing was different than I thought it would be. The judge went through every possible question to be sure Jesse knew what he was agreeing to, understood every aspect of it, and wasn't being coerced into this decision by anyone.

THE COURT: This paperwork tells me that you're going to plead guilty to count #11, which is criminal sexual conduct in the first-degree causing fear of great bodily harm committed on another person. Is that right, Sir?

THE DEFENDANT: Yes, Ma'am.

. . .

THE COURT: That is a felony charge. Do you understand that?

THE DEFENDANT: Yes.

THE COURT: And that carries with it a presumptive prison commit. Do you understand that?
THE DEFENDANT: Yes, Ma'am.

THE COURT: All right. Let's count with - We'll start with 85-CR-19-434. There's an added count two, the charge — To the charge of burglary in the first degree as to an occupied dwelling. How do you plead, Sir; guilty or not guilty?

THE DEFENDANT: Guilty.

THE COURT: And on 85-CR-19-435, count II, criminal sexual conduct in the first degree, fear of great bodily harm. How do you plead, Sir; guilty or not guilty?

THE DEFENDANT: Guilty.

JESSE TAYLOR ANDERSON pled guilty to first degree burglary from November 16, 2018 when he broke into my home to steal electronics and photos. He was indicted by a grand jury with eighteen felonies for events that took place that morning, fifteen of those being criminal sexual conduct charges. With the plea deal, he was convicted of one of those felonies: first degree criminal sexual conduct and he admitted to the aggravating factors. I was vulnerable, multiple acts of penetration, and my son was present nearby. These factors increased his sentence and prison time. If the case proceeded to a jury trial and he was found guilty of all fifteen charges, a conviction and sentence would be entered only on one charge because they were all related to the same incident.

He was sentenced to 250 months in prison. This equates to 20.83 years. Good time served would then drop it down to two-thirds of that: 13.875 years. Furthermore, he had already been in county jail since March of 2019, dropping it further down to roughly twelve years at the time of his sentencing.

I didn't realize they would run through things that happened that morning. I didn't realize they would detail everything. *But he admitted to everything.* Hearing him say, "Yes," he did those things and, "Guilty," was *amazing.* I never would have gotten that with a jury trial. A jury would have found him guilty, but here, he *admitted it.* I heard through the grapevine that he was telling people in county jail he didn't remember what he did. Well I do. *You know what you did. You recorded it.*

I broke down and sobbed when he was admitting everything because I was reliving it. Hearing his admission was validity that, yes, *He. Did. It.* Jake didn't console me because he had just gotten back from Florida, and because of COVID-19, he was wearing a mask and social distancing, and wasn't sure if he should come near me. He later did and regretted not doing it in the first place. I knew Cody wouldn't because he now had a girlfriend. So, I sat and sobbed alone, isolated. My mom stayed on the couch, but I was thankful she and I were mending our scars and we were back to being on good terms.

When everything was said and done, Cody surprisingly hugged me, and I fell apart. It was a tearful response of anger because 250 months wasn't long enough. It was a cry because it only started a new countdown for James and me—a countdown to when he'd be released from prison. It was a cry because we were finally seeing the end of a two-year battle.

Her head is down,
 Walking through the hallway.
 Don't notice her
 As she ties her shoe.
 She wishes she was invisible,
 In a crowd full of people.

But when it comes to her voice,
 She is a lioness.
 Hear her roar.

When it comes to words,
 She has something to say.
 Hear her speak.

When it comes to justice,
 It will prevail—
 And she will not back down.

You tried to silence her,
 But she is no longer the prey.

And you are no longer in control.

SHE IS THE LIONESS.

30

ON NEW YEAR'S DAY OF 2021, I WAS TAKING BACK MY POWER IN full force. I quit drinking. After that, I started taking Wellbutrin and it helped me control my anger. I'd always been resistant to taking depression medications, but it was finally time I would succumb to modern medicine and get medicinal help. I needed to for my son.

Soon afterward, I stopped feeling like I *needed* to drink all the time. I continued to have a drink socially if I was in the mood, but it no longer felt like a vice. I was in control again.

IN JANUARY I found out that in-person court cases in Minnesota would be pushed further out to mid-March due to a statewide order with few exceptions; therefore, sentencing in February would be via Zoom. There was no way I could let this happen. It was not registering in my mind as an option. I'd request sentencing to be pushed out further if I had to.

I was lucky enough to be able to receive my COVID-19 vaccination through my employer in the beginning of 2021. Claire knew how important it was for me to read my Victim

Impact Statement in person, so she asked if I wanted to formally request this to the court.

Oh yes, I do!

I wrote a letter to the court elaborating on a couple of things. First, my mom and I would be fully vaccinated for COVID-19 at the time of sentencing. I reiterated that the risk of transmission would be small because we were vaccinated, using hand sanitizer upon entering the building, and wearing masks. Second, I needed Jesse to hear me, see me, and feel my in-person presence with him. He could look away from a computer screen, like looking away from a movie. It wouldn't have felt as real, and I *needed* it to be so I could continue to heal, a small step into restorative justice.

The ending of my letter stated:

In a case with such an obvious perpetrator and a plethora of evidence, this would be an easily accommodatable step for something that will greatly benefit the survivor. I will never be fully healed, nor will I ever feel like the person I was prior to the attack. But this, again, is an easily accommodatable, safe step for my healing journey and peace of mind while the next countdown of my life begins: only twelve years of freedom with my son until he reaches his freedom from prison.

CLAIRE TEXTED me a week later letting me know *we would be able to have court in-person!* I was ecstatic. I was at work, so I could only be so excited without anyone noticing. I was given a gracious opportunity by Judge Leahy and the Chief Judge that would help me heal, move forward, and have better closure. Claire let me know my mom was able to join me, but I wouldn't be able to have any other support people with me due to COVID restrictions.

Despite the incredible feeling of gratitude for this opportunity, as the date neared, I became extremely ill again. I was experiencing stress-induced anorexia again. I was physically ill when I *did* eat, and I had insomnia and would sometimes only sleep a couple hours or less per night. But then I still wouldn't be tired during the day either; I felt manic. I was having anxiety and panic attacks, but still needed to maintain my job, hide all of this from my son, and still be a functioning seemingly normal member of society.

One good thing about insomnia and a racing mind was coming up with so many things to write down. I took notes on my phone during all hours of the night, and after a few days, I had damn near an entire speech ready to go to speak publicly after sentencing. I felt so productive!

"Dano, you're probably going to crash when this is all over," Erin said. We had been talking here and there and were starting to mend our relationship. I should have known the reason she wasn't talking to me much during the summer was because she'd read my texts mid-sleep in the morning hours because she was working overnight shifts and forget to reply later.

"Eh, I don't know. I hope I keep having this much energy. I've been accomplishing so much! And I'm not even tired during the day."

"I just wanted you to be prepared," she continued.

"Thanks, Sissy," I offered.

But what I discovered was all the feelings of mania, insomnia, anxiety, panic attacks, and physical illness would consume me up until the morning of February 10, 2021.

"She's not going to want to talk about what the plan is. She's going to want to take her truck. She's going to want to drive," my sister told Jake, knowing exactly how I would want the morning to go.

And she was right. I did want to drive my truck. I wanted to be in control of the vehicle, the road, the speed, the music, and where we were going. I needed all the power I could get. My mom and Jake rode with me to Winona that day, and my sister and her wife met us down there. My aunts, friends, ex-husband, and family watched via Zoom.

I HADN'T HEARD from Cody hardly at all over the last few months, particularly about the case.

We had to stop being friends once he got a girlfriend; our awesome co-parenting lifestyle was abruptly over. But when I angrily asked him why he had been supportive the whole time and then suddenly stopped, one of his responses was, "Because I didn't want to talk about it anymore." Those words took the breath out of me, the blood out of my heart, the life out of my soul. A small part of my heart died in that moment. But I later realized I couldn't be selfish and expect everyone to stick with me over the long, more than two-year process. Cody was starting a life with someone new, and me and my life moved to the bottom of the totem pole.

I WOKE up on the morning of February 10 with Leona at the foot of my bed and my kitties snuggled beside me. I took a shower, put my makeup on, and realized I didn't have an iron to iron my blazer and pants. Thankfully, Jake stopped at the store and bought one before coming over to my house. He ironed my clothes like an absolute pro and I put them on, ready to go. It was a dark navy-blue blazer with Wonder Woman liner inside and dark navy-blue pants. I know nothing about fashion, so I dug some old black heels out of my closet and put them on; good enough.

I drove to Winona that day with Jake and Mom and arrived around 1:00 p.m. My sister and her wife were already there waiting for us to arrive. They couldn't go inside so they went to watch on a computer at a nearby restaurant, and Jake met them after dropping my mom and me off.

I asked if I could have a police officer stand next to me when I read my impact statement. I kept having visions and anxiety over the thought of Jesse jumping across the table and being able to hurt me before anyone could stop him. The court graciously agreed to this as well, and it was determined Investigator Dungy would be standing next to where I would sit, and Investigator Loken would walk me up when I was called. Knowing it would be Dungy and Loken next to me felt like an absolute honor and subsided some of my fears about being in the same room as Jesse. I knew I was in a position where I would likely be making him mad, and that scared the hell out of me.

I was shaking, nervous, anxious, but ready.

"We will each have opening statements, then I will call you up to the stand. There will be a chair next to me with plexiglass separating us. You can take your time giving your statement." Ms. Galewski explained. I rolled up the sleeves of my blazer so the Wonder Woman symbol was showing.

"Is this okay?" I asked, showing Ms. Galewski and Claire the design.

"Oh, yes. That's awesome," Claire said. Ms. Galewski agreed that it would be no problem. I was thankful; it was subtle motivation.

I sat next to my mom, Claire, and Investigator Loken when the hearing started. I noticed there were multiple police officers in the room. I was surprised, but incredibly thankful. Loken whispered to me, "There are about ten to fifteen police officers next door watching this as well. They are all vested in this case." I put my head on her shoulder and thanked her. What she didn't know at the time was that I was not only thanking her for telling me that, but also for saving our lives, protecting us, spending countless hours on this case, and being an amazing human being, the same as I felt about Dungy.

Ms. Galewski started the sentencing by saying what Jesse thought about my statement, "It was mostly bullshit." He had made a phone call from jail, which was recorded stating this. I was frustrated he was able to read it beforehand, but in the big picture, it didn't matter. Shortly thereafter I was called to read my statement. I brought my inhaler because my throat was closing; it was hard to breathe. Anxiety was consuming me. I sat down next to Ms. Galewski with plexiglass surrounding me when Judge Leahy asked if I needed a glass of water.

"No, thank you, Your Honor."

I pulled the microphone closer and began...

31

On the night of November 17, 2018, I sat down on the couch after cleaning up remnants of the day and curled up with a glass of Pinot Noir. It was an awesome day. My son and I had gone to see *The Grinch* in the theater, bought Christmas lights for the tree and listened to Christmas music on the way home. We went to the gym in St. Charles and I got him an ice cream cone from A&W for being a good boy. He knew that when the clock showed the seven o'clock hour, we would watch one episode of *Paw Patrol* before bed. After we did, I tucked him in with my pink book light clipped to the side of his bed, his Paw Patrol night light shining colorful paws on the ceiling, a touch night light, his glowing iguana named Sheldon, and his soft yellow blankie. After his bedtime routine, I finally got to relax. I had looked at the lock on the front door to make sure the dead bolt was turned the correct way indicating it was locked; it was. I checked to make sure the garage door was closed, and the lights were off; they were. I checked to make sure the patio door was locked; it was.

I snuggled on the couch with the cats on my lap and

scrolled through my phone. I texted my usual friends and sipped my one glass of wine next to my glowing Christmas tree. Shortly thereafter, I went to bed feeling safe and whole. I was happy.

As a fellow survivor once described, *"I was happy while someone was waiting to hurt me."*

At 1:27 a.m., I woke up to a noise at the end of my bed. A moment later, a gun was pointed at my head and I was being yelled at to not move. Before I knew it, I was lying on my stomach with my wrists zip tied together behind my back extremely tight; but I could hardly register the pain over the fear that I felt. Over the course of the next five hours, I was raped three times, had my life threatened, had my son's life threatened, all while uncontrollably shaking and crying in fear after being held hostage in *what used to be* the comfort of my own home.

How do I describe shaking hysterically for five hours, wondering when it would end and if I'd be alive to see the sun rise? How do I explain how it felt to be held down, tied up, and raped? I couldn't scream. I couldn't run. I couldn't hide. I couldn't go anywhere; I had to stay there for my son. I had to stay quiet for my son. How do I explain what it felt like to have my three-year-old child's life threatened while I was tied up and could physically do *nothing* about it? How do I explain what it was like to have my child, the one person I would give my life for without hesitation, ask why a man hurt his mommy?

Afterwards, I had to put on one of the biggest acts of my life when my son looked at the marks on my wrists from the zip ties and asked why. How do I describe what it was like to lose my home, my town, my safety, and my security? My life was completely uprooted, and I lost the happiness and light I once had in my soul. I slipped a few important things into my purse, threw on my coat, and took one last look around knowing it might be the last time I'd ever set foot in that house again.

How do I describe how it felt to look at every single man I passed for the next three and a half months wondering if he was the man who raped me, wondering if he was the man looking to kill me? I didn't want to step outside for fear that someone was watching, listening, waiting – just as the man, whom I now know to be Jesse Anderson, had promised. I had to cart my child around in between homes with our belongings packed in a garbage bag and a laundry basket. I had to take $760 worth of HIV prophylaxis medications that could have caused kidney failure, liver issues, and death. I had to take a morning after pill in case the unknown, masked rapist impregnated me.

How do I explain what it felt like to have my entire life gone through by a group of people I didn't even know? My house was on display; it was a crime scene. I cried out all my tears, so when my heart wanted to cry more, nothing would come out. I had to sit my son down and explain to him that even though we couldn't be at our home in St. Charles for Christmas, Santa would still find us.

I'd like to ask if Jesse Taylor Anderson could even fathom how any of this would feel. Or how he'd react if it happened to his wife, or one of his two daughters – or to himself. I bet he couldn't imagine it. I bet he also couldn't imagine that I am a survivor, and I am far stronger than he thought I was. He broke into the home of a warrior.

Thanks to him, I lost a promotion, my house, my car, and my trust in humanity. What was he thinking when he loaded the clip in his gun that night; the one he held to my head? Did he think at all about his beautiful wife and children? Did he think about how he was *in my wedding*? Did he honestly think I'd be able to make snow angels with my son in the morning as though nothing had happened?

Your Honor,

I was a school nurse for three years. After switching my

career to the best clinic in the nation, I was promoted to one of the four charge nurses after six months. Less than eighteen months later, against the normal standards of the institution, the department created a position making me the permanent, full-time charge nurse. I am prompt, efficient, ethical, organized, and am strongly supported within my department. I now lack any motivation to continue education in nursing. Instead, I fight with feeling broken, used, abused, damaged, and unworthy. I spend a lot of time in a state of rage that takes so much energy to tame it enough to get through the day. I've put so much time, money, and effort into making sure my son and I can feel safe, but none of that brings back the sense of safety I once had. I will never be who I used to be. But what I do know is I've always been strong enough and smart enough to protect my son. Like a lioness, I will always protect my cub.

I didn't deserve this, nor did my son. My son now is obsessed with bad guys. It's a constant reminder that he endured something no child should have to endure or watch his mom suffer through.

I wake up every morning and think about how I almost died in the middle of the night after going to bed feeling safe and sound – back when *I was happy*. Every day I am grateful to wake up without a gun in my face. I think of my son and whether he is safe. And then I ask myself *why* my mind must do this every single morning. Jesse Anderson threatened over and over again to murder my three-year-old little boy if I told anyone what he did. So much so that I *didn't* tell the police. It was five long, painful hours of him threatening me not to – in return for my son's life. It was my mom who met me at the grocery store that morning after we escaped the house. She called the police (thank God). My mom has endured the toll of being a secondary victim.

If I hadn't cooperated like I did that morning, if I had put up a fight, I would instead probably be a missing person or a murdered person and my innocent little boy would be the same. I have told friends of mine who know Jesse, "When he gets out of jail, he will find me and he will kill me." Not one single person has denied that statement. Even though he's now living behind bars, I live in fear.

Why me? Why did he target me? How did he find out where I lived? This was obviously premeditated. He had called my ex-husband a few months before and asked, "So you and Dano are officially done now, right?" Was that him getting permission? What did I do to deserve this? He video recorded himself raping me. How many times did he watch that video? How many times did other people watch that video? Was it sold online? How many times were the most private parts of my body exploited on the worst morning of my life?

I can hardly describe how this has affected my family and me. For two years I have been silenced. I had a falling out with my parents. I had a falling out with my sister. I've pushed my ex-husband Cody away. I cried myself to sleep and woke up with nightmares that haunt me the rest of the day, but I bottle it up and hide behind my usual smile. I take my rage out on people who do not deserve it. And for that, my friends and family, I am so, so sorry.

Because I am so broken, I keep people at a distance. My soul feels black. Sometimes I cannot control my anger and pain, and it scares me. **Hurt people hurt people.** Who have I become?

I'm no longer who I was, nor will I ever be that person again. But I must take this and try to make good use of its energy. So, I'm part of the Survivor Advisory Group to the Governor of Minnesota. This year is my second of two terms. I attend a sexual assault support group in Olmsted County, and before COVID-19, I extended support group on an informal level to be sure my fellow warriors would never feel alone. I am an activist and an advocate and I always will be. It is now who I am.

We're here today because he found a mistake on a search warrant. A win for him. We're here today because a plea deal was the "safe route," vs. trial and because the DNA, the videos he recorded raping me, my shorts found in his truck, and his first statement were all in question due to search warrant technicalities. But I was not high. I was not drunk. I know what he did. It is fixed in my memory. I know my story. I told my story. And it was proven true by the videos he took.

He told his wife he was going on a hunting trip. That wasn't a lie. *He hunted me.*

It takes four pounds of pressure to pull the trigger on a 9 mm handgun. I think about this every day. Four measly pounds of pressure could have ended my life when that gun was repeatedly pointed at my head. Four pounds of pressure and I wouldn't be here today. Four pounds of pressure and I wouldn't have been there to watch my son go to his first day of kindergarten or see him lose his first tooth. I wouldn't feel the warmth of his little head on my chest as he listens to my heartbeat, and he wouldn't have me to lay my head on his. Doing this is our proof to each other that we survived and we're still alive.

It was extremely tough for me to sit down and finalize this statement. I have avoided it until the last minute, because this statement will never be final. I'll never fully heal, never get over this, never forget. Today as I near the end of this statement, know that this is not the end. This is not where my broken soul heals. But it is the start of a new chapter and my mission to advocate for other survivors who have endured rape and sexual violence.

So here we are. He wears a mask, and I am shaking – just like the last time he saw me. But today I am shaking for new reasons, with a new energy. As Dr. Maya Angelou says, "...you may kill me with your hatefulness. But still, like air, I'll rise. I can be changed by what happens to me. But I refuse to be reduced by it."

Your honor, Jesse Anderson's sentence is my sentence too. His sentence is my son's sentence. While we're already in hiding as much as we can be, I don't know what we're going to do when he's out. It's been a countdown to get to being here today. But it only starts a new countdown – until he is released from prison.

994 out of 1000 rapists walk free. Please don't let him be one of them.

Danielle Louise Leukam

32

WHILE I THINK JESSE'S SENTENCE SHOULD HAVE BEEN LONGER and I have absolutely no sympathy for where he's put himself, I have been thinking about Jesse's *family*. They are grieving too.

I met with Jesse's ex-wife after sentencing. I found out a lot of things that happened from her perspective over the last two years that made me realize she was a victim too. There were multiple things she told me that if minor details had transpired a little bit different, it could have immensely changed the outcome. I don't have permission to talk about the plethora of things she told me, but our visit was heartbreaking yet healing. It was incredibly eye-opening, and we've formed a new, strong bond that will keep us tied for life.

She mentioned he was going on a hunting trip down to Rochester in November of 2018. He almost didn't leave, but she encouraged him, "No, honey, you should go. You deserve to go on a hunting trip." His black Under Armor sweater was thrown away, which was why it was not found as evidence. And all of the women Jesse was cheating on his wife with looked like me... big brown eyes and long brown hair. It's terrifying to be "his type." Despite the lies he told her, she *knew* in her heart when she heard me bring up Stockholm Syndrome that what I was saying about her ex-husband was true; it was something he joked about with their children.

She kissed Jesse goodbye the day he was arrested, not realizing it would be their last kiss. But not only was it their last kiss, it was the end of Jesse's income and support for her and her kiddos, and his first ex-wife and their kiddos. There are gaps in resources for sexual violence victims, secondary victims, and families. While filling the gaps for survivors is a burning passion of mine, filling the gaps of lost income, child support, and resources for families who were left behind after an abuser was incarcerated is a passion as well. His family and children did not deserve the heartache and loss that he caused. It's a work in progress, but my long-term goal is to start an organization that can fill that gap.

Keep in mind when you say hateful things towards perpetrators, you may be affecting the family who was left behind. If you say, "He has rapist eyes," please know his children may have his eyes. Please know there is a family grieving as well and it wasn't their fault.

Some of his family/friends were thinking, perhaps because of what Jesse and/or the attorney was leading them to believe, *Was it really* that *bad?* My answer to this is, please see chapters one through thirty-one. Being pink on the shoulders after a day in the sun isn't that bad. Dying your hair auburn and having it come out orange isn't that bad. Getting into a fender bender and breaking a headlight isn't that bad. Why? Because things that aren't *that bad* are fixable and can go away leaving behind no evidence, changes, or scars.

Have you ever seen the YouTube video of Brandt Jean hugging Guyger, the police officer who shot and killed Brandt's brother Bothum in his Dallas, Texas apartment? A friend sent this video via email and when I watched, I cried a spiritual, inspiring, deep cry I had never felt before. I cried out of envy. I cried because Brandt Jean was able to forgive his brother's murderer. I cried because I can't see myself reaching these feelings towards Jesse. I cried because I wish I could feel that freedom and allow such a forgiveness. While this case was completely different than mine because Jesse's actions were premeditated, calculated, and he is not remorseful, I envy the freedom of how forgiveness may feel.

OVER THE SUMMER of 2019 James was playing with some new toys. He had some plastic pieces from a build-a-truck toy (the kid could be an engineer someday) and he thought it would be fun to play with handcuffs. He asked me if he could put the plastic pieces around my wrists and I said, "No!" abruptly. I felt awful that I had such a harsh reaction, but I apologized and explained that mommy doesn't like playing that kind of game. No zip ties in mommy's house, and no handcuffs.

I'm far more cautious and willing to ask for an escort when unsafe situations arise. For example, I was walking into a store in the summer of 2019 and a guy in the car next to me said, "Damn, girl! Damn, girl! Come here! Where you from? Don't I know you?"

I turned around and said, "No," and kept walking.

He continued, "No, wait! Don't I know you from high school or something? Come over here!"

"No, and no," and I went inside. I was bothered. I made sure he didn't follow me in the store. I quickly grabbed what I needed and made my way to the checkout.

After checking out, I had one of the store cashiers walk me to my car. I didn't feel safe going back out alone because I blew this guy off and didn't give him the time of day he was hoping for. Who knows what he was capable of? Who knows what anyone is capable of? I didn't want to guess; I didn't want to take chances. Thankfully, he was gone by the time I went back out.

I WILL NEVER AGAIN BE who I was prior to this assault. Do I want to be? Nope. Not only was the trigger pull four pounds of pressure, the pressure of trying to stay alive and the fear I endured brought out the lioness in me. I went through hell but came out stronger than I was before I went in.

Everywhere I go, I have pepper spray, a knife, self-defense keychains (one for each pocket), and if I can, my German Shepherd. Everything I do has to be mindfully thought through to be sure I am doing it in the safest way possible. I make note of where exits are and my surroundings in general. Are my doors locked? Windows locked? Where is the dog? Where is James? Who is walking by my house? Whose footprints are those?

I miss the fall of 2018. I miss the way I felt. I miss the happiness I had, the contentment, the way I felt after Sober October and going to the gym three to four days a week. I miss the innocence I had. I miss the life I had before that morning. But I'm glad to be stronger today.

I am haunted by his name. It terrorizes my life. One of the things that scares me the most is, *What if he convinces someone in jail to find me and kill us when they get out?* As an FYI, it was difficult typing that last sentence, because now I feel like I'm putting an idea into someone's head. I live cautiously because I don't know who he is capable of convincing outside of jail to do something awful. It consumes my thoughts every single day, and despite feeling free with court being over, I still will never truly and deeply feel safe again.

I try to convince myself to be hopeful though. I can't tell you how many times in the last six months I have said, "Seize the day." Despite my dark clouds, there's always sun shining behind them. I have said, "Seize the day," to my friends and family; I have preached it. I have felt it, through my skin and deep down into my bones, because who knows if you're going to wake up tomorrow? Who knows if there will be a tomorrow? You don't. So *live*.

IT WAS A LONG TWO YEARS, and I'm thankful the court process is finally done. I was silent during that time and am thankful to finally be able to use my voice. While I preferred the thought of going to trial and him ending up serving life in prison without, or even with, the possibility of parole, I know the prosecutors did what they thought was best. But still, nothing will ever be good enough to bring back what I've lost.

I still have unanswered questions, such as, *How did the meth get in my system? Was he using something to disguise his voice? Did he take my Apple Watch?* But I am guessing these questions will remain unanswered.

Sentencing only started a new countdown for my son and I: the countdown until Jesse gets out of prison. Until then, I'll continue to live fuller days, striving for goals and dreams I never would have before. Life on the other side of suffering is beautiful.

Some people talk about their cancer, some people don't. Some people talk about their divorce, some people don't. Few people talk about rape, most people don't. Thus, survival stories, healing journeys, outcomes, and perpetrators are not talked about. I'm ready to fight, to break that trend, and to bring awareness. **Rape culture needs to end.** We, as parents, should teach our children about consent and respecting women and all humans (she/he/they) and to not **objectify** people.

One person's story may be someone else's survival guide. If my story would encourage healing for even one person, then sharing my story with the world was worth it. I don't want sympathy; I want allies. I don't want to be noticed for what happened to me; I want to be noticed for what I'm going to do about it. I couldn't put up a fight that morning, as I was held hostage with my son being used as a pawn for my cooperation, but I sure as hell can fight now.

More accountability needs to be put on the perpetrators. When we think of rape statistics, we think of how many **women** get raped and how many **women** get sexually harassed. **Women** need to be safe; **women** need to not be objectified; violence against **women** needs to end. Well yes, this is absolutely true. But what about the statistics of men who are rapists? What about the statistics of men who are perpetrators? What about holding them accountable? Exploiting them like they exploited us? We need to focus more on the problem: **the abusers.** Women can try their best to *not* get raped, and obviously that hasn't been good enough. So it is time to focus on the problem. It is time to focus on prevention. I'm saying men and women here based on statistics, but it is important to know that he/she/they rape and assault he/she/they. It goes all ways. This includes children as well, unfortunately.

What can we do? Love our children. Teach our children consent. Listen to your children. **Men** (and women), watch your friends. Watch your family. Call them out if they're not treating a woman right. Call them out if they're doing something concerning. Get them help. Turn them in. Report as a bystander. **Stop the rape jokes.**

MY ADVICE to others who know a survivor is to be supportive, be there, be present, and be available. If the survivor you know is anything like me, it's unlikely they'll ask for help. Don't forget about them. Ask him or her how they're doing and if they need anything. Find resources for them; find resources for yourself. If they have kids, offer to take the kids for a day so they can rest or write or read or exercise. Let them talk. Listen.

What has become hard is when people hear my story, sometimes I hear about their story I didn't even know they had, in return. There are more stories than I would have ever imagined there could be amongst my family and friends. There are stories I know only few details about, stories where the perpetrator was not served justice, and stories that were untold to the authorities.

I grew up around the corner from a boy we'll call Jay. One day when we were little, my sister, Jay, and I were riding our bikes in the neighborhood. One of the older boys from up the road took me and locked me in his parents' shed in their backyard with him. I was screaming and crying, but he wouldn't let me out while his friends watched.

My sister and Jay threw rocks at their bikes and upset them enough that he finally let me out. As soon as he opened the door, I ran as fast as my little legs would take me, brushing against the corn field, to my parents' house, hysterical as I made it inside.

Jay died by suicide in 2010 after being raped. He was incredibly kind, and he and Erin saved me that day over twenty years before. And I wasn't there to save him when he needed me. I wish I had been.

IN THIS JOURNEY, I feel like my eyes have been opened to beautiful souls. I never had materialistic goggles; I never saw people for what they had and their status in life. Hell, I grew up borderline lower middle class and still am. But I have a mom with a heart of gold, a sister with a heart of gold and fire, friends with beautiful souls, and that makes me the richest person in the world. I don't believe *all* people are truly good at heart like Anne Frank, but many people *do* have beautiful souls, and *that* is what I am drawn to.

But as expected, it's not all beautiful... sometimes I find

myself completely numb. Sometimes I am completely selfish. Sometimes I don't care who walks out of my life because maybe they weren't meant to be in it and didn't care enough to fight to stay. Some days I want to lie in bed all day under the covers and hide from the world mindlessly watching Netflix, crying alone watching *Grey's Anatomy* and *Station 19*. But those days aren't often and despite *wanting* to do that, I *can't* do that as a single, working mom. Time is the most precious element, and I don't have much to spare. Besides, the sun rises and life goes on and I want to live it and experience it with this second chance I've been given.

Fight, flight, freeze, but as Stevie Crosiant and WeAre-HER.net reminded me, appease is the fourth. That morning, I appeased Jesse. I cooperated, and that must have been the right decision because we're still here today. As survivors, we can hide, survive, or thrive. It's not just one of those three that we will become, it's a rollercoaster that we are on, going up and down through our healing. I'm just building my rollercoaster to stay on the upwards track.

Seize the damn day.

FAST FORWARD TO JUNE 24, 2021. On this date, Jesse entered an Alford plea to 3rd Degree Criminal Sexual Conduct (from allegations of sexually assaulting a vulnerable adult at a group home where he worked) and Aid and Abet Theft of Firearm in Willmar, MN. He had been charged with nine counts of felony theft of firearm, stealing guns from the home of a man he had done work for because he was unhappy with the pay he received. The plea means he does not admit to the facts of the case, but acknowledges there is sufficient evidence to convict him, per the KROC news article.

Sentencing was June 25, 2021 and I learn his 153 month (twelve years and nine months) sentence for 3rd Degree Criminal Sexual Conduct and 21 months for Aid and Abet Theft of Firearm sentences will be served concurrent to the prison sentence he received for attacking me. While I had a heads up that this would likely happen, I still wonder how the vulnerable adult feels about this. Is it fair? He was also ordered to serve conditional release of ninety-nine years after release from custody. Conditional release is similar to parole and is sometimes viewed as a less restrictive alternate to hospitalizing psychiatric patients, per Wikipedia.

Later on June 25, I drove with my uncle to his cabin three and a half hours away. I heard funny, surprising, and eye-opening stories on this drive. While we were talking about what age we started drinking, I mentioned that even when I did drink in my twenties, I rarely let myself get drunk in public because I didn't want to be vulnerable. Upon saying this, he said my Aunt Lisa says the same thing about her younger years. This was important to me before I had been sexually assaulted and it was important to my aunt without having been sexually assaulted too. This is one of the *many* reasons I am so angry that I was raped. These actions are required for women because our society teaches us how to avoid being raped when it needs to teach men to stop raping. It wasn't even *so I wouldn't be raped,* it was simply the life I was living.

WATCHING James sleep at night with the glow of his night-light iguana still illuminating his cheeks, watching his chest rise and fall with every breath, has been the ultimate comfort for me. Though I'm still reminded there is evil in the world, the peace in my son reminds me of the beauty of living.

I often wonder if this book is my threat to humanity. Will this book tell the world the story of that morning, in addition to the four other sexual harassment and assault incidents I endured prior to this event and say, *I'm. Fucking. Done. Do. Not.*

Mess. With. Me. Anymore.? Is that what it says? Part of me hopes so. But the other part of me hopes it will instead be my gift to humanity. I hope that it shows people who have gone through similar situations that you *can* come out on top, on the other side. You *can* be a warrior and a lioness, and you *can* come out better than what you were before. Your abuser does not own you. You own you. Love yourself. Take back the control; take back the power. You've got this—*We've. Got. This.*

Networking, such as going to a support group, has been incredibly healing for me. I understand a large number of people don't talk about being raped or assaulted, but it is incredible the support you may receive if you do. Networking with other survivors helped me normalize the feelings I was having and it helped me to not feel as alone.

The blame for what happened to me is not on an establishment, his parents, his wife, me, my lack of having a dog at the time, or my lack of having a roommate. The blame is on him. HE is a rapist. HE is the perpetrator. HE did this to himself. HE did this to me. HE exploited me in countless ways, including the pictures he stole and did who knows what with, the video he stole, and the video recording he made and at one point had on Porn Hub.

I am forever linked with this man. I cannot make that go away. I cannot forget. To avoid being hurt again, I push people away but I'm working on this. I am responsible for my own healing and happiness, and as I type these words, I continue to push forward and find the woman I was meant to be—and that makes me happy.

I have big dreams of public speaking that I have proven I *can* do despite my love for being left alone and my excellent skills of pushing people away, and writing books. Regardless of my isolation and introvert personality—well, more introvert than extrovert anyway—I have a message to give to the world.

Hear me *roar.*

. . .

AT THE END of the day, I don't believe there is such thing as "getting over it and moving on." It is more of... adding chapters to your life you didn't think you would have to add, that highly influence the rest of the book and the rest of your life. We must learn from those chapters and help others learn too. It is now part of me and because of that I will live differently. He did not defeat me.

2018 was the year I lost my spirit, safety, security, and comfort. It was the year I had to take down my Christmas tree before Christmas even happened. It was the year I was held hostage for five hours, thought I was going to be murdered, and had to listen to hours of threats against my son's life.

But it was also the year I realized that life is short, and I need to do what makes me happy. I need to do the things I wished I had done when the gun was at my head, when I thought I was going to die.

2018 will forever be the year I did not let him conquer me. 2018 is the year I survived.

EPILOGUE

April 10, 2021

2:58 a.m.

I hear the metal sound of a doorknob clumsily jiggling. After a moment there is a click and the door opens, a familiar sound. The bed squeaks quietly as my German Shepherd sits up, suddenly on high alert. I hear shuffling of little feet across a small stretch of carpet, then a small stretch of wood flooring in the hallway, and again on carpet in my bedroom. By this point, I am on high alert as well, waiting for my little man to moan and groan, pulling his way up onto my bed. His little hands grab my new gray blanket, and he hoists himself up. He crawls up to the pillow right next to mine. I welcome him by pulling down my blankets and sheets, making a special spot for him to snuggle. Once he has settled himself, I cover him up, hug him tight, kiss him on the cheek and lay back down after gently listening to his heartbeat.

Thump-thump, thump-thump, thump-thump.

My dearest son,

I know one day you will come across this book. One day you will realize what happened to mommy the morning "a man was fixing our shower." There are parts of me that will be broken forever, but know that you are the reason I am still here. You are the reason I was strong enough to keep us alive. You are the reason my heart still beats. You are my everything.

You may be grown up, heading to college, or having children of your own by the time you come across this book. But darling boy, I needed to protect you that morning, as I had every moment prior to that, and every moment since. This public book is one thing I cannot protect you from. I can no longer hide what happened, but I hope in reading these words, you know we moved on with our lives and we overcame the terror of that morning.

I always wanted what was best for you, as I still do while you are reading these words. If you ever feel not good enough, not strong enough, not courageous enough, let me know, and I will tell you how much love I have for you and how proud I am of the man you've grown up to be. In every moment that passed when you were a child, I somehow grew to love you even more than the moment before.

Lion cub, I've taught you consent, I've taught you to respect all humans, I've taught you to not objectify people the best that I could. I've taught you to watch your friends, notice if they're not treating a woman right, notice if they need to be called out on something. Teach my future grandchildren the same and together we can make the world a safer place one human at a time. Despite how small that seems, it means a world to an unknowing victim who doesn't have to become a victim.

There's no way to adequately write the words to explain my love for you. There's nothing I could write that could ever be enough. Instead, I will spend the rest of my life fighting for you, protecting you, and loving you.

You are the reason my sun shines, my heart beats, and my lungs breathe. I would do anything for you, still. I will always do everything in my power to keep you safe. There's no love in the world more

*than a mom's love for her child. I have all the fight in the world inside
me to keep you safe. And I am ready, as always.*

I am a lioness. I am Mom.

ALL MY LOVE,

Forever and ever,

Mom

ABOUT THE AUTHOR

Danielle Leukam has loved writing for as long as she can remember. When she was raped in her home in 2018, she was inspired to write her story to raise awareness and help other survivors. Amid writing her memoir, she started a website to blog, wrote a second book containing twelve sexual assault survivors' stories, wrote a children's book, and started a thriller.

Danielle is from the Rochester, Minnesota area and works as a full-time charge nurse. She is a writer and blogger, a survivor and advocate against sexual violence, and is on the Survivor Advisory Group to the Governor of Minnesota.

Danielle has taken back her power and she hopes to empower other women to do the same. She hopes her memoir and compilation of survivor stories will be a survival guide for women. Danielle loves to hear from readers!

To stay up to date on my work and progress, subscribe to my mailing list at www.danielleleukam.com.

www.facebook.com/daniellelouiseleukam
www.instagram.com/danielleleukam
www.twitter.com/danielle_leukam
www.patreon.com/daniellelouiseleukam

ACKNOWLEDGMENTS

Anne, Anna, Jenny, Jordan, Katie, Jake, Cara – for being my best friends through thick and thin. Erin, Cody, Amy, Mom, Dad, Lisa, Wells, Lynn, Dan, Paul, Debbie, Cassey, Kris, and Phil and the rest of my family. Tessa, Logan, Renee, Laura, Elyse, Leah, Heidi, Colleen, Don, Holly, Dr. Leibovich, Dr. Gettman, Dr. Thompson, Dr. Gearman, and the rest of my amazing family at work. Adam, the Krenzkies (Kaila and Brandon), Kassie, Erin, Laura, Ashley, Brian, TSM, Owen, Sherry, my mom's coworkers, SANE nurses, Mark, Kate, Winona County and St. Charles PD, Claire, Christina, M.Z., Gina, Shayne and Becky, my realtors Ryan and Jodi, Rochester Women's Shelter, Women's Resource Center of Winona, Steve and his amazing ice cream, the employee at the Verizon Wireless store who respected I was "Jane Doe," and Allen Eskens. Also, Gracie Wright, you matter. You matter to me.

To the angels God sent me along the way,
Mark Dungy, Kate Loken, Claire Exley, Christina Galewski, Ann
Wilson, M.Z., and Jake Socwell, thank you for showing your

kindness, support, and patience with me. You've helped me get to where I am today.

*Please visit **the Boutique Station** in Rushford, Minnesota owned by Amy Engelhart, an amazing woman that supports survivors and honors Sexual Assault Awareness Month.*

And to Stanger Construction, LLC, thank you for your wholesome generosity.

I have a sincere and special thank you to all of you, my dearest friends and family, who have been supportive of me through this healing process. I wouldn't have made it out of the hole I was in if it weren't for my co-workers; thank you for your respect, support, and understanding. And putting up with me, of course. It would take one hundred pages to express my gratitude for everyone. But in summary: Mom, thank you for coming back to me. Thank you for being an incredible role model and mother. You are Memaw Lioness, the strongest woman I know. Auntie Lisa and Uncle Wells, thank you for taking me in on such short notice and always being loving, accepting, and taking me under your wing. Auntie Lynn, who can make me see the light in any dark situation, who never has a hurtful thing to say, and is one of the kindest people I know, thank you. And Uncle Dan, we have far more in common than just the name.

Erin, you are my hero and you always have been. Thank you for everything you sacrificed to support me. Thank you for being an incredible human, (as proven by the love that your army kids have for you). My world would be nothing without you.

Thank you to Jane Ashley Converse and Dennis Vogen (local authors, check out their books!). Thank you for letting me pick your brain in asking you endless questions about this whole process. I appreciate your willingness to share your expertise!

Thank you, sincerely, to the law enforcement of St. Charles and Winona County. You have saved my son's life and my life. I will forever be grateful and indebted to you. Investigators Dungy and Loken, I owe you my life. You two will do great things; you already have, and I am forever grateful. Winona County is lucky to have you. Oh, and I think we need to add a Vikings vs. Packers game to our agenda.

Claire, Ms. Galewski and team, thank you for putting up with my ups and downs, tears and rage, and irrational thoughts. Claire, you are *incredible* at what you do. Ms. Galewski, you are going to continue to do great things. Your brilliance and professionalism will take you far.

Jenny, I would be nothing and nowhere without you. Thank you for your patience, support, and flexibility. Also, thank you for having basically the same brain as me (except mine lacks a photogenic memory) and being an amazing friend. I'm Pinky and you're Brain.

Drs. Leibovich and Thompson, thank you for giving me a safe home for my son and I to live in during such a traumatic time of our lives. Thank you for groceries, generosity, kindness, and support. Dr. Gettman, thank you for your encouragement. And Dr. Elliott, my day would be boring without your humor. Thank you for your guidance.

SANE nurses, for those who took care of me, and the rest of the SANE nurses out there: Thank you for all that you do! I was blessed to have an *amazing* SANE nurse.

B.L., a fellow survivor—stay strong. You got this.

M.Z., you are an amazing human. Thank you for your support and guidance. You made me feel safe, cared for, and you didn't forget about me. Your colleagues struck gold in having you on their side.

Cody, thank you for coming home and being an amazing father to our little boy. I couldn't do this without you, nor do I want to.

Jake, thank you for having been my ride or die. Thank you for being my number one fan. Thank you for being the bridge that got me to the other side; it is quite lovely over here. You were the best friend I ever had.

Owen, thank you for having the same mind as me. How can this be? I'm blessed to have such an intellectual friend who graciously leads me to be better at what I do.

Anna, you are an incredible human and I admire your free spirit, thank you for being there for me for the last... fifteen years? Wow, we're old! Same with Jordan... eighteen years? Hot damn. Anne, for the next hundred years; how did I get so lucky as to have you in my life? And thank you to Katie (the girl who got me my first journal) who has been my support, coach, friend, and informal editor. Katie, you are one of the smartest people I know, and I'm blessed to have you as a friend. Thank you for your time, commitment, and support. Now let's travel to Paris!

To the rest of the humans in my world who have deeply touched my heart and helped me through these terrible years, *thank you.*

A special thank you to donors who helped to make this book possible:

The Boutique Station in Rushford, Minnesota
Stanger Construction, LLC.
LeRoy's Auto Sales & Collision Repair
B.L., Cabbi and Becky, Eric, Joel, Trace, Elyse, Jenny, Jake, Jesse, Sharon, James, and Lindsey, Lee, Eric

Beta Readers: *Katie Herbers, Anne Ulwelling, Anna Schmidt*

ARC Readers: *Anna Schmidt, Terra Carroll, Stacie Sell, Sherry Irvin, Caroline Hill, Mel, Cassey Nguyen, Kaila Krenzke, Amanda Olson, Jan Turbes, Nikki, Stevie Croisant and We Are HER, Kristine Oelkers, Ashley Kramer, Jessica Tilford-Machuga, Dinorah Bond, Dr. Candace Granberg, Sherrie Wolbeck, Kristie Shorter, Shawn Schmidt, Crystal Weber, Brianna Evers, Owen, Cara Ristau, Logan Knapp*

"You don't need to be brave when you're writing. You need to acknowledge that you're terrified and do it anyway." – Roxane Gay